BUS

✓

GLOBAL EXPANSION
IN THE INFORMATION AGE

GLOBAL EXPANSION
IN THE INFORMATION AGE

Big Planet, Small World

T H O M A S   J .   H O W A R D

VAN NOSTRAND REINHOLD

I(T)P™ A Division of International Thomson Publishing Inc.

New York • Albany • Bonn • Boston • Detroit • London • Madrid • Melbourne
Mexico City • Paris • San Francisco • Tokyo • Toronto

Copyright © 1995 by Van Nostrand Reinhold

Published by Van Nostrand Reinhold

I ⓣ P™ A division of International Thomson Publishing, Inc.
The ITP logo is a trademark under license

Printed in the United States of America
For more information, contact:

Van Nostrand Reinhold
115 Fifth Avenue
New York, NY 10003

International Thomson Publishing Gmb H
Königswinterer Strasse 418
53227 Bonn
Germany

International Thomson Publishing Europe
Berkshire House 168-173
High Holborn
London WCIV 7AA
England

International Thomson Publishing Asia
221 Henderson Road #05-10
Henderson Building
Singapore 0315

Thomas Nelson Australia
102 Dodds Street
South Melbourne, 3205
Victoria, Australia

International Thomson Publishing Japan
Hirakawacho Kyowa Building, 3F
2-2-1 Hirakawacho
Chiyoda-ku, 102 Tokyo
Japan

Nelson Canada
1120 Birchmount Road
Scarborough, Ontario
Canada M1K 5G4

International Thomson Editores
Campos Eliseos 385, Piso 7
Col. Polanco
11560 Mexico D.F. Mexico

1 2 3 4 5 6 7 8 9 10   QEBFF   02 01 00 99 98 97 96 95

Library of Congress Cataloging-in-Publication Data

Howard, Thomas J.
    Global expansion in the information age : big planet, small world / Thomas J. Howard.
    p.   cm.
    Includes bibliographical references and index.
    ISBN 0-442-01932-7
    1. Information technology—Economic aspects.   2. Technological innovations—Economic aspects.   3. International business enterprises.   I. Title.
    HC79.I55H69   1995
    658.5'14—dc20
                                                94-44554
                                                CIP

To Linda
For the first 27 years on our journey to forever
together

To Jack and Katie
For giving me the chance to experience the joys
of parenthood

To Mom and Dad
For teaching me to ask questions

Contents

Foreword

Nobody knows international business like Tom Howard does. He lives it, breathes it, talks it, and now writes about it. In the pages to follow, Tom shares two decades of the study and practice of doing business internationally. He gives you a special focus on how to do things better with information technology. And, in the rapidly changing information-empowered world, people who can do business faster and efficiently will win.

Tom tackles both technology and business issues with a delightful and sometimes irreverent flavor. Moreover, he knows how to behave well internationally. He's helped me expand my business to Europe, Asia, and South America and to avoid disastrous goofs in getting started.

He once stopped me in my tracks and cut out some

clip art from a presentation I was taking to Japan. Inadvertently, I had used a picture whose background looked remarkably like the Japanese Navy flag flown during World War II. "Hummm," he said, "Don't dredge up old bones, Currid. Find some different art."

Tom also saved me from blushing embarrassment when we had a visitor from England. He gave me his 30-second explanation of the difference between England, Great Britain, and the United Kingdom just before I put my foot in my mouth.

In each chapter of his book, Tom provides wonderful insight into doing business outside one's homeland. He opens with a little anecdote, discusses the issue at hand, then closes with how you can apply technology to make things go better. He shares wonderful nuggets of knowledge.

All in all, Tom has given us two books in one. First, he gives us a well-paved path for putting together a business plan using the information highway. And, second, he posts road signs so we'll know when to take caution over cultural differences and when to speed ahead. This book should become required reading for anyone venturing outside of the continental United States to do business.

Cheryl Currid
President
Currid & Company

Introduction

What has changed in your world today? Surely something has changed. Everywhere we look, we see change. And you don't have to look very hard to find it. Just pick up the newspaper. There are lots of stories of local interest that are quite important to us in our personal lives. The political stories are great entertainment.

What changes really affect the way we do business? The chances are good that what really impacts our business lives involves changes outside our own country. Maybe it is increasing trade friction between the United States and China. Maybe it is a political assassination in Mexico. Perhaps it is the attempted merger of European automobile manufacturers.

This book is about the world. It is about change. It is about how you can turn those changes into opportunities for the global expansion of your business. And it is about how you can use technology to make it all happen.

Let's go back a few years to get a good example of global expansion in the face of change. Look at Attila the Hun. He may not have been such a bad guy after all. Maybe he wasn't a paragon of virtue. Sure, he was a little rough on his employees and a little aggressive toward competition. His experience, however, is not totally worthless to the reader of history. He followed one principle that is as true today as it was 1500 years ago. Expand your business and grow.

Since this is the introduction to this book, let's introduce ourselves to the subject matter—the world. Take a minute and go grab your atlas or globe. Go ahead—I'll wait . . .

Now, look at our world. What do you see?

The earth is a big planet. It is almost 25,000 miles in circumference and weighs 6.6 sextillion (that's 20 zeros!) tons. The total surface area is about 200 million square miles. That's a very large ball!

When people first started exploring our planet, it took a long time to get from one place to another. In the thirteenth century, Marco Polo took about three years to go from Venice to China. In 1492, Columbus took about 70 days to travel from Spain to the Bahamas.

Today, the world is a much smaller place. You can fly from New York to London in three hours on the Concorde. More important, in this age of information, technology allows us to talk instantly to anyone, anywhere, anytime. You can communicate anything you want at astounding speeds with a previously impossible level of reliability.

It is, indeed, a small world.

Because of the capabilities provided us by technology, it is impossible for any developed nation to make a political decision, take an economic action, or precipitate a social change without having a serious impact on other developed countries.

The same can be true for any major commercial enterprise because, in today's environment, it is more and more apparent that competition is, indeed, global. Technology has made the instant world possible. What can we do with this capability? Take advantage! Expand your business and grow!

First, the opportunities for profitable growth in international markets are legion. The fastest-growing market for many products and industries is often outside the United States. So, the potential for revenue and profit is appealing. Sobering the appeal of this opportunity is the threat of competition. Other companies are global in scope; in dealing with the world rather than just a few countries, they enjoy the economies of scale.

Next, many customers are global companies, and they want to do business with a company that can support their requirements for goods and services around the world.

Finally, there are companies with international operations that are in various stages of disarray. Not only do they not provide growth opportunity, but they don't even make money. Reengineering is in order.

This book provides you with a useful guide on how to expand or improve your global business—and how to use technology as the powerful tool it can be. The book is organized along the lines of a business plan and follows that logical flow. In each step of the "plan," we discuss the appropriate application of technology.

A REVIEW OF THE CHAPTERS

In the first chapter, we discuss the world of information technology (IT). Information technology provides us with some of most important tools we have in dealing with change. From something as commonplace (though not at all simple) as a fax machine to highly sophisticated wide area networks (WANs), businesses hum with the power provided by instant information. Just a few years ago, much of the information we now take for granted wasn't available at all, much less in an instant.

Reason would suggest that the companies best positioned to utilize the tools of technology are those that provide the products and services that technology affords—the computer manufacturer, the software developer, the electronics manufacturer. Surely, these people know how to use what they sell. Fat chance! Remember the shoes of the cobbler's children? Many companies that understand technology and what it can do have little or no understanding of how it can be used to manage their business outside the United States.

How about the company that sells delivery services? There's a real opportunity! A company like this is driven to differentiate services that have reached the commodity stage of development. How would you like that challenge? And, yet, look at United Parcel Service (UPS). By innovative utilization of technology, information about any customer's shipment is readily available to anyone who needs it.

The possibilities of expansion are exciting. Almost immediately, however, the hard facts of the world of international business hit you right between the eyes. Before investing a lot of time and resources to devise a plan that misses the target, some casual tire kicking is in order —an attempt to put the opportunity and cost in some reasonable perspective. Every day, as you pick up the newspaper or read a periodical, you see more evidence of change. Business processes change. Technology changes. People and attitudes change. In Chapter 2, we discuss change and how it affects everything we do.

In Chapter 3, we explore some initial thoughts on how to approach the problem of expansion. We address such questions as what you have to gain from an expansion, how to begin, where to find help, and how to apply technology to the process. Taking these first steps can help you make a tentative decision on whether it is even possible to expand your business.

Developing the world's great markets is a piece of cake compared to the problems you'll encounter in the internal process of deciding to become a truly international company. So, what does a company need to do to come up with a winning formula for globalizing its business?

In Chapter 4, we discuss ways to do the internal selling necessary to make the international efforts of your company successful. We describe how change will require internal reengineering, and we describe how you can make those changes in your business.

It is amazing to see how companies spend large amounts of money developing very sophisticated products or programs to address markets about which they know little or nothing. Although their business model may have worked quite well in the United States, the cookie cutter usually doesn't work.

In Chapter 5, we suggest ways to identify credible sources of market research information and a down-to-earth approach to gathering the necessary information to proceed with the project.

It is in this research stage that technology helps the most. Tapping into public databases will provide valuable insight into what's going on in the target industry outside the United States. Here you will find out who are the database providers and what software is available to make this stage a lot easier.

Once you have a good understanding of the market requirements for the products, distribution, promotion, and pricing, you'll need to ask yourself what the key success factors are for your company.

The offering you have, whether it is a product or a service, must be good or your company would not exist. It doesn't matter whether you sell the most sophisticated widget that the world needs to survive or whether you sell watchbands. Technology either drives or supports what you do and makes it good.

Now the task is to see if that "goodness" can transfer to the foreign market that you have now spent time to understand and to find out what changes are required.

In Chapter 6, we deal with how to determine real product requirements and what you do with them. There will be many examples of how—and how not— to develop products and services.

Distribution mechanisms are very different from country to country. Since efficient distribution is so key to a successful business, it is critical to devise a distribution plan that works not only for the product but also for the country in which the product is being distributed.

In Chapter 7, we cover various techniques for understanding distribution channels and how to get the right answer from the right level in the organization. Then, we look at how you select from the various alternatives to choose the best distribution strategy for your product in the territory.

Your company may have the greatest product in the world, but communicating the proper message to the prospective consumers is, of course, key to success.

Every country has its own set of communication tools. Languages are different, and concepts do not always translate well. The cost and effectiveness of various media vary from country to country.

In Chapter 8, we describe several tried and proven methods of defining the right communication strategy, from picking an agency to choosing a media plan that is effective and meets the budget requirements.

In all the world's markets, value is a key factor in the purchase decision. The buyer, not the seller, defines value. So, in establishing the pricing strategy, you must explore the entire value proposition. That includes price, margins for the distribution channels, and factors such as warranty and support capabilities that affect the life cycle of the product.

In Chapter 9, we discuss the aspects of a pricing strategy: positioning, manufacturing and distribution cost structure, hidden costs, and pricing.

The financial plan involves the most effort and complexity. The financial requirements and expectations of doing business globally are significantly different from those of doing business in only one country. Determining how the business model will change is critical to the success of the whole venture.

The range of financial and legal issues is very broad but these matters are fundamental to the entire decision process. In Chapter 10, we describe the issues and suggest useful ways to deal with them.

Nothing runs without human resources. Dealing with human resources in foreign countries is very different, however. This is not to say that the skills developed in managing people in the United States don't apply; they do. There are, however, significant cultural and legal differences that will affect the plan.

In Chapter 11, we explore ways to find, attract, compensate, and motivate people to manage the international business, both at home and abroad. Further, we give some very useful tips on how to get the rest of the people in the organization singing out of the same songbook. Finally, we provide ways to set up the communications—both telecommunications and interpersonal communications—links that are so vital to a global business.

Now that the plan is complete, we look at a few nuances of working in an international environment. In Chapter 12, we answer questions like: How do you give your business card to a Japanese executive? In France, why doesn't anyone answer the phone in August? and How come nobody showed up for the meeting I scheduled for 10:00 a.m. in Panama?

In Chapter 13, we review what we previously discussed: establishing the corporate structure, finding the right people to staff the operation, prospecting for distributors or representatives, looking for financial alternatives, and dealing with import/export regulations. In other words, developing the market.

Technology does not stand still. Companies must have processes that comprehend that fact. We will conclude with a discussion of how you keep in touch with new developments in technology and how those new gadgets will really make a difference in the bottom line.

After reading this book, you will be much better prepared to decide what to do with international opportunities and threats. And you will have a much better idea of how to take advantage of the opportunity to expand your business.

1

The World of Information Technology

Have a look around your office or your company. Do you notice anything peculiar? Probably not. And that's the story for this chapter. In the office today, we are surrounded by technology, and nobody notices.

Today's business professional uses computers, fax machines, cellular telephones, voice-mail systems, E-mail systems, scanners, and CD-ROMs. And the list goes on. We take it all for granted.

The ubiquitous computer is here. It is on the desktop. It is at home. It is on the airplane. It is powerful. It is connected to huge databases of valuable information.

INTRODUCTION OF NEW TECHNOLOGY

The rate at which technology is introduced is accelerating. It took almost 425 years from the invention of movable type by Johannes Gutenberg in 1445 to introduce the typewriter in 1868. It took only 34 more years (1902) to introduce the electric typewriter.

The abacus has been around for thousands of years. The first calculating machine was introduced by Charles Babbage in 1834. The first digital computer (ENIAC) came out in 1946. The first Apple Personal Computer (the Apple I) was announced in 1976.

One key reason for this acceleration is that development of technology feeds on itself. One invention or technological breakthrough creates hundreds of other products.

The invention of liquid crystals provided a technology that could make displays on personal computers smaller and flatter. Further, the new displays required relatively low levels of power. Availability of this technology, along with other developments, paved the way for the notebook personal computer.

Notebooks, introduced in 1990, by virtue of their size and portability, are carried somewhere, usually away from a place where you can conveniently plug them into an outlet—to an airport, a car, a conference room. Available battery technology was sufficient for low-featured PCs for short periods of time (from one to two hours). The real requirement for a battery-operated fully featured PC, however, was six to eight hours of battery life.

Today, we have a notebook PC that can do almost anything a desktop PC can do. It can run for six to eight hours in full operation (many more in standby mode) and can hook up to a network to become an extremely powerful tool.

This all happened within the last five years!

ABSORPTION OF NEW TECHNOLOGY

The rate at which we absorb new technology is also accelerating. It took 20 years after the introduction of the telephone for the first million users to be connected. Broadcast television was around 11 years old before 1 million people tuned in. There were more than a million VCR owners after only six years. Four years after introduction, there were 1 million cellular telephone subscribers. Since its introduction in 1981 by IBM, there are more than 250 million PCs installed around the world!

A key reason for this acceleration is that, as each new technology is introduced, it is easier and more intuitive to use than its predecessor. Remember the first VCR you bought? Did you ever figure out how to program the @#$* thing? Compare that to the VCR of today. You just say to the machine, "Record, Wednesday, 7:00 to 8:00 p.m., Channel 5." That's easy to use!

One feature of any successful new product is that it has a useful purpose. The user, however, must understand the problem to be addressed before technology can help. Therefore, the broader the target user group for the product, the more successful it will be.

There are more than 500 million telephones installed around the world because everyone has an understanding of what a telephone can do for them. There are somewhat fewer rocket telemetry simulators in use because of the limited number of users who actually understand the issue being addressed by such a product.

Sometimes, the intended use for an invention is very different from its actual or primary use. For example, the radio was originally intended to be a wireless replacement for the telegraph, not an entertainment medium. Clever users who are motivated to fix a problem or create an opportunity will use whatever technology is available.

There are a few negatives about technology that we need to consider. Some of the things technology enables us to do are not always desirable. Networks don't get installed as easily as we would want. The satellite link goes down halfway through the transmission of a very large file. And, sometimes, technology is a tool for criminal behavior. Recently, a federal grand jury indicted a college student for using university computers to distribute pirated software over the Internet.

For years, companies have tried to automate their work processes. Many of them just went out and bought a bunch of computers and threw them at the problem. The result was a bad process that sometimes ran faster. The challenge for us is to apply technology intelligently to the problem or opportunity, whether it is reengineering our business processes or expanding our business outside the United States.

Although there are many different areas of technology that are interesting—space exploration, medical science, biotechnology—here we focus on information technology (IT). More specifically, we focus on those areas of IT that relate to the global aspects of business.

Certain core technologies are fundamental to creating and running an international business. These are the building blocks on which all other technologies depend. They are:

1. Networking

2. Database

3. Personal productivity software

If you don't have these tools, go get them. Without them, you will not be able to conduct your business effectively in the future. Let's explore each technology and what it can do for your business.

NETWORKING

Networks provide a mechanism to connect company resources. No technology is more useful and satisfying than a properly designed and managed network. Nothing is more wasteful and frustrating than a poorly designed and managed network. The choice is yours.

A network doesn't just connect computers; it connects people. A well-designed and well-managed network provides a conduit through which people and workgroups can collaborate across functional lines, geographic boundaries, and time zones. It connects people within a company. It can also connect suppliers and customers to your company.

The so-called information superhighway is a supernetwork. It connects many different resources in order to make information available to a vast amount of people. It couples private intercompany networks with commercial networks available to the public. Examples of such commercial networks are Internet, CompuServe, NiftyServe (in Japan), America On-Line, and Prodigy. There will be more discussion of the information superhighway later.

If you already have a network in place, it is a good idea to review what you have. The objective of this review is to assure availability of network connections to people regardless of where they are—in the office, on the road, at a local or regional office, in an airplane, or in a hotel room.

The network contains many different and interrelated pieces:

- A "pipe" through which data flows—the wire in the buildings, the telephone line from the hotel room, the wireless connection from the car
- Intelligent hubs and routers—the devices used to connect several networks together
- A network operating system
- Gateways to the outside world of public or private services, mainframes or minicomputers, and any number of resources required to run the business
- Tools
  Administrative tools to manage network user information
  Management tools to distribute software
  Diagnostic and monitoring tools to check devices hooked to the network and to monitor traffic flow

DATABASE

A database is a collection of information organized in a useful way. This is a simple concept but a profound idea. A well-designed and well-managed database provides multiple users, in multiple locations, access to information at the time it is needed. A well-designed and well-managed database can become the most valuable asset of a company.

Databases come in many flavors, differentiated by the location in which processing is done. The host-terminal model, for example, does most of the processing at the host. The file server model puts processing at the client location but stores the data at the server location. The client/server model allows the client and the server to share in an optimum way.

The important thing to remember about a database is that it requires careful planning and execution. You cannot overemphasize the importance of good planning and design. Pick the database tool most suitable for your company. It probably supports structured query language (SQL) and employs the client/server model. It will have many third-party development tools available. It will provide gateways to a wide variety of applications from many different vendors.

TOOLS

Tools are those applications that sit on the desktop or mobile PC and provide personal productivity as well as connectivity to other people and resources. The basic toolbox looks something like this:

- Spreadsheet

- Word processor

- Presentation graphics

- Filing system

- Calendar

- Access to the outside world

If you haven't already discovered this, you will soon find out that everyone has an opinion about which tool is best. You will never resolve this inherent conflict. Accept that fact, and get on with developing a strategy that will work best for your business. Here are some things you should consider:

- Be consistent. You don't want to waste money, training, and support resources on every possible application that becomes available at the local computer store. Microsoft Windows™ provides a consistent look to the user from a wide variety of very different applications. The spreadsheets, word processors, graphics packages, and other tools have a similar look and feel to the user.

• Because many jobs involve many different tasks that tend to run parallel with one another, make sure your toolbox allows the user to move from one task to another very easily. The user wants to be able to stop typing a report and check the calendar to see if a meeting has been confirmed. Sometimes, an E-mail message is urgent, and the sender wants to interrupt the receiver who happens to be working on a presentation. Most Windows applications have the ability to switch easily from one task to another.

• Finally, these tools should be able to share data from one to another. For example, you create a presentation that needs a graph of some data that are in a spreadsheet file. You may be working on a report that requires some information that is in a database on the network. This data should be easily transported from one application to another.

SECURITY

All the power and capabilities of a network, a database, and desktop tools raise the issue of security. Although this is not an exhaustive look at security on a network, a few words are in order.

One of the most valuable assets of any company is the knowledge it possesses. A lot of this knowledge is resident on a network. The nature of a network allows

for access to that information by many people. Therefore, some attention to the protection of that information
is desirable. There are many ways to secure that information from unauthorized access.

- You can provide some level of security by requiring
  one or more levels of sign-on clearance before any
  user can get on the network or into a specific file.

- You can encrypt the data so that a specific "key" is
  required to unlock it. The "key" can be made very
  secure. A word of caution here: There are severe
  limitations to the movement of encrypted data
  across national borders.

- Auditors require accountability. They ask lots of
  questions about the things they are checking: Who,
  what, where, and when? There are many tools
  available that make this information accessible in
  order to insure accountability on the network.

ENABLING TECHNOLOGIES

The last area of technology we discuss here involves
those technologies that enable the business to create and
manage a global enterprise. After the network, database,
and tools are installed, what are the applications that
help us address those issues inherent in a global business? Here are some technologies that make international business easier.

Mail Systems

Where would we be today without interoffice mail?
How can we communicate with our fellow workers? We
can't. Every company has some sort of "mail" system. It

may be as simple as yelling across the room at a co-worker and as complex as distributing thousands of pieces of paper to locations around the world.

Voice-mail and E-mail systems merely apply technology to the concept of interoffice mail. These mail systems communicate from one or more workers, either by voice or in writing.

By using IT, mail systems break down the barriers of time zones and the "he's in a meeting" wall. Now, by typing an E-mail message or orally creating a voice message, senders can send mail, with attachments if necessary, when they want, to as many people as they choose. Receivers can read or listen to the mail whenever they have the time.

Document Management

A large amount of information can and will be created in any network environment. The more users there are, the more information is generated. The real trick is to know how to get to the desired information when and where it is needed. That is where document management systems help.

Documents, which can include letters, faxes, E-mail, spreadsheets, and images, are prepared, indexed, and stored in a predetermined way. Then they can be retrieved using the identifiers that make sense to the user, such as author's name, date, key words, or subject matter.

Document management systems allow for all geographical resources to be treated as one. In other words, users don't care where information was created or where it is stored—they just want it right now!

Workflow

Workflow management systems are closely aligned to document management. Workflow software is a tool to create the paperless office. Don't wait around for the paperless office because it isn't coming. The wasteful and inefficient use of paper, however, can be minimized. Automation of sequential processes such as filling out a purchase order can be dramatically improved through workflow automation.

This technology is particularly important for the global company. Just ask the salesperson in Milan who needs an expense report signed by the regional manager in Paris, who then sends it on to London for payment. Using workflow software and the right internal procedures, that process can actually flow quite smoothly.

Groupware

The modern company that is organized around processes rather than tasks usually operates in cross-functional teams. Groupware technology makes the location of any team member irrelevant. With the appropriate use of groupware products such as Lotus Notes or DCA's Open Mind, the group can use information in a collaborative way to achieve a desired result.

Groupware products tend to be very good at sharing information across many different boundaries, such as organizations, time zones, and languages. Groups can work on the same information at the same time through the use of electronic discussions. Groupware products have many features found in workflow and document management—storage and retrieval of documents, key word searches, and remote access.

Mobile Computing

The exigencies of business today demand that people work away from their traditional offices. Traveling workers need access to information. They need to be connected, which can involve tasks as simple as looking up the status of a purchase order or as complex as calculating the construction costs for a petrochemical plant in some foreign country.

Technology has made mobile computing possible. With the availability of very powerful, very small PCs and with the continued development of communications capabilities—both wired and wireless—the mobile worker can now be connected to the source of information anywhere in the world.

Wireless computing is important not only for the mobile worker but for the headquarters worker as well. Wireless connections of computers in a building or on a campus eliminate a lot of problems in working with older buildings or campuses and complexes that stretch across public highways.

Geographic Information Systems and Global Positioning Systems

Geographic information systems (GIS) arrange data according to some prescribed geographic point of view. For example, if you want to know the sales volume of a particular product by country and by city within a country, a GIS system is essential. These systems are very useful in providing sales forecast information and tracking performance of a particular sales region.

Global positioning systems (GPS) allow the user to find the physical location of something anywhere in the world. If a taxi driver in Tokyo needs to get from point

A to point B—not always a straightforward assignment —a GPS system in the car will set out a proposed route.

Both these technologies are important for the global business because they provide information by location. They will eventually become essential in managing resources on a worldwide basis.

Electronic Commerce

The hassle of sending pieces of paper from one person in the company to another can be managed well with the thoughtful use of all the technologies already discussed. Electronic commerce opens that same capability up to people outside the company. There are several products that allow companies to interact with one another electronically.

An ATM is a classic electronic data interchange (EDI) device. Another example is a system that allows customers to enter their orders onto their vendors' computers. No purchase orders to get lost in the mail. Fewer mistakes in data entry. No pricing errors. The same systems can be used to issue invoices and pay those invoices through bank transfers.

These capabilities present some unique issues with regard to information and fund transfers across national borders. These issues will be discussed later in the book.

Multimedia

Multimedia refers to the marriage of sound, video, and computing technology in an application or a set of intermixed applications. Presentations, education, or training are some common uses of multimedia technology.

In the global business, multimedia technology can

provide very useful tools to communicate complex concepts in a multiple of languages. By adding the French sound track to the English version of the video description of how to repair a power supply in a computer, your training manager can effectively communicate with the field technician in Paris.

EXAMPLES

This is a lot to throw at you at one time. Let's look at a few examples of how some of these technologies work in the real world. Of course, there will be many more examples as we move through this book.

In the fall of 1983, I was working at Compaq Computer Corporation, preparing products for introduction into Germany and the United Kingdom. Some of the warning labels inside the machine had to be translated into German.

The most modern technology available at the time was a wire service based on the old teletype. I sent a telex containing the English version of the label to the technical director in Germany. He translated it and sent it back via the same mechanism.

The problem was that the telex transmission allowed only capital letters. If I applied the English rule of capitalizing only the initial word in a sentence, the result would not make sense to a German reader. In German, all nouns are capitalized. In English, we sometimes put words in all caps for emphasis. This is not done in German.

The only way to fix this problem was to mail the label to Germany and have it translated there and mailed back. There were no worldwide couriers in 1983, so that the whole process took two weeks.

Today, there are several options provided by technology. The most readily available is the fax machine. Today, fax machines all over the world talk to each other routinely. A fax takes about 30 seconds and costs about $3.00.

The drawback here is that there is redundant data entry: The English version must be initially created, the German version must be typed in Germany and retyped again in the format required by the printer. This can lead to mistakes. At the very least, it causes redundant editing in a language probably unfamiliar to the editor. But, it takes less than two weeks.

The other option is E-mail. Just type a message to the technical director in Germany, attach the file that contains the text of the label, and send it over the network. In Germany, the technical director makes the changes to the file and sends it back. This takes a maximum of one hour and, since the network has a dedicated line to Germany, costs almost nothing to send.

The German version of the original file can then be sent to the printer immediately for typesetting with no further data entry.

Let's look at another example. M.W. Kellogg entered into a contract with Maraven, the Venezuelan national oil company, to expand a refinery in Port Cardon, Venezuela. The team members on this project were in Houston, Texas; Clinton, New Jersey; Etam, West Virginia; Port Cardon, Venezuela; and Valencia, Venezuela—not a close-knit group geographically.

Rather than spending time and money moving people and information around from location to location, M.W. Kellogg set up a network. Over this network, the team members—and others—have virtual meetings. On a real-time basis, they share data, video, voice, and text. The right people with the right information can be in the meetings at the right time.

This was not a trivial system. It cost about $6 million.

It took time and effort to install. But, over the life of this contract, it is projected to pay for itself in staff time and travel expenses alone. The real benefit, however, is that people can share information and make decisions, regardless of where they are. That is an incredibly powerful tool.

This, then, is an overview of some of the technologies that can be used in an international enterprise. In the next chapter, we discuss change—change in business, change in technology, and change in people—and how these changes affect your globalization efforts.

2

The World of Change

When I was growing up, my father offered me some sage advice. "Work for a big company," he said. "They'll take care of you." He now thinks I am an itinerant, shiftless job-hopper because I have had three jobs in 30 years.

Consider this. *BusinessWeek* (May 9, 1994) provides this list (Table 2.1) of large organizations and the number of jobs they have eliminated since the first quarter of 1991.

Table 2.1 Job Cuts, Jan. 1991–Dec. 1993

Company	Jobs Eliminated
IBM	85,000
AT&T	83,500
General Motors	74,000
U.S. Postal Service	55,000
Sears	50,000
Boeing	30,000
NYNEX	22,000
Hughes Aircraft	21,000
GTE	17,000
Martin Marietta	15,000
DuPont	14,800
Eastman–Kodak	14,000
Philip Morris	14,000
Procter & Gamble	13,000
Phar Mor	13,000
Bank of America	12,000
Aetna	11,800
GE Aircraft Engines	10,250
McDonnell Douglas	10,200
BellSouth	10,200
Ford Motor	10,000
Xerox	10,000
Pacific Telesis	10,000
Honeywell	9,000
U.S. West	9,000

Table 2.1 represents almost 624,000 people who have been forced to make major changes in their lives. And, of course, that's not all. There have been many smaller changes.

My father is not stupid and he is not ill informed. His advice was good advice 30 years ago. But I am not so sure it is the advice I would give my son. Why? Because things have changed. Things are changing.

Everywhere we look, we see change. Every newspaper reports on it; every weekly or monthly periodical analyzes it. Business is changing, technology is changing, and people and attitudes are changing. All the rules are changing. And nowhere in the world is change more apparent than in the world of international business. Our challenge is to understand these changes and anticipate their impact.

OUR RESPONSE TO CHANGE

When you are confronted with change, you have some choices to make. You can resist it, you can accept it, or you can embrace it. Your choice will have a profound impact on you and your company.

To illustrate the alternatives presented by change, let me offer the American automobile industry as it faced the threat posed by the Japanese. At the beginning, in the 1970s, the industry resisted change. The Big Three automakers had a lock on the distribution channel. There seemed to be no way a foreign competitor could get into the channel and compete effectively.

As Japanese automakers smashed that assumption, the U.S. makers still resisted. They ran to the government for protection but didn't look within themselves to find the root of the problem.

Next, during the 1980s, the American automotive industry began to understand that their competitors made better products, with more features wanted by the buyer, better quality, better fuel economy, and not necessarily a lower price. They responded with smaller, more highly featured cars with significantly better quality. All of a sudden, Japanese market share gains in the United States began to slow.

Finally, during the 1990s, the U.S. industry embraced the changes in the market. They saw a different buyer with different criteria for purchasing a car. They changed their model. Now, features and quality became the focal point of product development. The manufacturers enhanced their relationship with their distribution channel. Their pricing became very competitive. They gained market share back from the Japanese makers.

Certainly, I don't mean to imply that the shift in market share over these three decades was totally a result of the U.S. auto industry's modifying its approach to change. It is clearly not that simple. But there were fundamental changes in the industry's way of looking at the market and its approach to change, which contributed to the rebound.

Before we look at making your company a global enterprise, let's look at change and how it will impact your plans.

Let's first examine the changing world of business. Entire industries are undergoing dramatic changes. Just look at the banking industry. The lines of distinction are very fuzzy. What is the difference between a bank and a savings and loan association? Where do you go to borrow money? To save money? To maintain a checking account? How about the stockbroker, accountant, or life insurance agent? Many "financial advisors" are now licensed to provide all three services.

The computer industry of today is very different from the computer industry of just 15 years ago. It used to be IBM and the seven dwarfs. Today, IBM is against the ropes. Mainframes look like dinosaurs, and personal computers are no longer just personal.

For 70 years, IBM has run on three basic beliefs: Pursue excellence, provide the best customer service, and show respect for the individual. Louis V. Gerstner, the CEO of IBM and the first outsider to run IBM, wants to change that. He has eight new principles.

IBM's New Principles*

1. The marketplace is the driving force behind everything we do.

2. At our core, we are a technology company with an overriding commitment to quality.

3. Our primary measures of success are customer satisfaction and shareholder value.

4. We operate as an entrepreneurial organization with a minimum of bureaucracy and never-ending focus on productivity.

5. We never lose sight of our strategic vision.

6. We think and act with a sense of urgency.

7. Outstanding, dedicated people make it happen, particularly when they work together as a team.

8. We are sensitive to the needs of all employees and the communities in which we operate.

The old-timers are going through culture shock. But Mr. Gerstner is convinced that fundamental change is required for survival.

Coca-Cola and Pepsi-Cola have been battling each other for years. They have a cozy little rivalry and keep on selling colored water for a lot of money. All of a sudden, we see products like Snapple and Gatorade making some significant inroads into the refrigerators of America.

---

* *The Wall Street Journal,* May 13, 1994, page 1.

BUSINESS IS CHANGING

There are many attributes of business today that are different from the past. To characterize some of these differences, we've employed the following catchphrases:

- Global competition

- Glued and unglued

- The instant world

- Knowledge-based

For the past several years, we Americans have been pretty comfortable in our competitive position at home. The Europeans have been very busy with their own problems with recession, unification, and movement toward "Europe 1992." Well, don't get too comfortable. Look at corporate profit growth in a few key European countries in recent years, as shown in Table 2.2

Table 2.2 Growth In Corporate Profits in European Countries, 1992–1994

Country	'92–'93 Growth (%)	'93–'94 Growth (%)
United Kingdom	+29	+25
France	−19	+32
Germany	−24	+39
Italy	−11	+49

Source: BusinessWeek, May 2, 1994.

With this growth in profits, European companies can be stronger in their own markets and more aggressive in their export markets. You may find a new list of competitors here at home as Europe continues to dig itself out of recession.

On the other hand, U.S. companies are expanding to markets outside the United States. They meet new competitors in the new markets. And, as companies expand to international markets, they change internally. The rules—the policies and procedures—have to change to accommodate their new business. The products change to meet new requirements. There are new problems to face: currency hedging, communications in different languages, countertrading.

Industries are in a constant state of flux. The defense industry is consolidating. Since the end of the Cold War, we don't need as many companies feeding the Pentagon. The computer industry, after a decade of fragmentation, is beginning to consolidate. There will be fewer computer companies in the future.

At the same time, many companies are ungluing themselves. As the business grows, each business unit needs greater visibility. Divisions are created. In some cases, divisions are sold off because they no longer support the goals of the parent business.

We live in an instant world. We can communicate anywhere in the world instantly. We lack the patience for any other condition. Things have to happen fast. It is now a world of survival of the fastest, not necessarily the fittest. The company first to market with new technology has a competitive edge.

Today, we face a new paradigm: We are a knowledge-based world. Knowledge is the currency of the future. The company that knows the market best, understands the technology best, and knows the distribution channel best will succeed. The person within the company who has the knowledge necessary to succeed will move up the corporate ladder. We are a world of "knowledge workers."

The costs to employ a knowledge worker—salary, benefits, and overhead—are going up, while the costs of technology—computers, communications equipment, and software—are going down. This phenomenon drives a change in the way we look at those resources in our companies. Competition is constantly introducing new low-priced products and services. As a result, we must look constantly at tasks that can be automated. Automation provides a way to improve productivity of the more expensive human resource.

For example, using voice mail and E-mail means the sender of the message does not have to wait for someone to answer the phone or call back. The receiver doesn't need a support person to write down the message. Those valuable human resources can be doing things computers can't do.

BUSINESS AND TECHNOLOGY: THE DRIVER AND THE ENABLER

Several forces drive business to change. Here are a few:

- The move to globalization

- The requirement to manage risks better

- The need to be first to market

- Growing demands for customer service

- The necessity for cost containment

You must face one or all of these requirements in your business every day. Technology provides us with tools that enable us to meet these needs effectively. In Chapter 1, we discussed some of these enabling technologies: networks, databases, and tools.

The drivers—the business demands—and the enablers—the technology—create a regenerative loop. The more demands are placed on technology, the more tools technology provides. The more tools available, the more problems can be fixed.

TECHNOLOGY IS CHANGING

If you think the world of business has changed, you ain't seen nothin' yet. Technology is changing at blinding speed. We are in the middle of a technology evolution that looks very much like a revolution. The information technology industry is fundamentally different from the way it was 15 years ago. The price/performance ratio of computers is improving dramatically. We have moved from closed, proprietary, hierarchical systems to an open client/server architecture. Technology is significantly easier to use than it was just a few years ago. And we can get information anywhere at any time we need it.

All those new trends we looked at in the business world are placing demands on the technology to provide tools that meet the demands. The business needs demand that we empower and enable people to do more. Therefore, we provide them with desktop and mobile network nodes that give them the spreadsheets, the word processors, and the databases they need to do their jobs.

Traditional company organizations are changing. We tend to work more with teams of people who have the necessary skills and knowledge to achieve the desired result. It doesn't matter where those people work or in which organization they are assigned. Companies tend to organize their teams in terms of results much more than in terms of function.

In Figure 2.1, for example, instead of an engineering department and a manufacturing department and a mar-

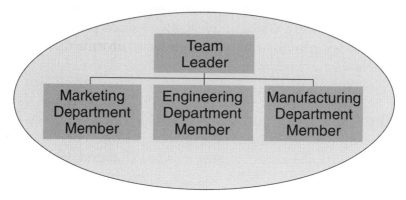

Figure 2.1 The product development team.

keting department, there is a product development team. Each member of the team, although organizationally assigned to a department, works as a member of the product development team.

We use the virtual corporation today. People who do not work for the same company collaborate on projects. Once the project is over, the people go on to the next opportunity. This gives the business the best available resource to do a specific job without the burden of keeping that person gainfully employed after the job is complete.

In each of these trends, teamwork and the virtual corporation, technology has provided the help required. Groupware, mobile computing, workflow and document management systems, E-mail, and teleconferencing are some of the tools available to teams that help them achieve results.

PEOPLE ARE CHANGING

As business trends continue to place demands on technology, the information technology industry will respond. Using the tools will become easier, more intuitive, and the results will become more predictable. And the tools will provide the needed information any time, anywhere.

This means, of course, that people will have to change. Their attitudes toward technology must become more open. They must accept technology more easily; they must resist it less. They must become more computer-literate. We are seeing this attitude adjustment in the younger generation today. They are very comfortable with computers and technology. But they are not the only ones. As businesses downsize, more mature and experienced workers are forced to learn new skills. They must accept the value of technology.

The technology industry must also cooperate. It must set the right level of expectation in the mind of the user. In 1994, pen-based computers cannot recognize hand-writing well enough to replace a piece of paper and a pen. Users should not be led to believe they can. In 1994, on the other hand, a user can sit down at a PC and type. The result can be edited and printed and can be made to look very good. Maybe pen computing will make this easier in the future. Maybe voice recognition will make it even better and easier. But that is the future, not now.

Change, then, is fundamental to our lives and the world in which we live. In the chapters that follow, we discuss many aspects of doing business internationally. As you move ahead with the development of your plans and strategies, remember the element of change in everything you do.

In the next chapter, we discuss some ideas for gathering a bit of information and making a quick assessment about the global future of your company.

3

Understanding the Opportunity Through Some Casual Tire Kicking

You are now sitting in your office or at home just thinking about all the great opportunities offered by international expansion of your business. But, almost immediately after that initial thought, the questions start.

- Why should I expand outside the United States?
- How do I begin?
- Where should I look for help in understanding what is involved?
- How do I apply technology to the process?

Before investing a lot of time and resources in devising a plan that misses the target, some casual tire kicking is in order. This should be an attempt to put the opportunity and cost into some perspective that has some meaning for you.

In this chapter, we discuss some initial thoughts on how to approach the problem. Answers to all the questions we've listed here will be developed so that you can make a first-pass, gut-level decision on whether it is even possible to expand your enterprise.

WHY SHOULD I EXPAND OUTSIDE THE UNITED STATES?

Will your business be improved if volume increases? Will your business be better if you improve your cost of goods? Do you have customers who want your products delivered and supported in countries outside the United States? Do you have competition?

If the answer to any of these questions is yes, then you have a reason to expand your business outside the United States.

Volume

The most obvious reason to grow any business through geographic expansion is to increase volume. By expanding the scope of your efforts, you will sell more things, make more money, and absorb more overhead. There are some subtle advantages to geographic expansion compared to other methods of increasing volume.

One way to increase volume is to broaden your product line. Regardless of whether you sell goods or services, you can make more varieties of what you sell and offer them to your existing customers. Assuming, however, that limited resources prevent you from expanding your product line, you may consider instead using those resources to enter a new geographic market.

If you chose to sell more kinds of goods or services to your existing customer base, you have the advantage of a prequalified prospect list. The drawback is that you are limited to the life cycle of that product or service. Once the existing customer base or market is saturated, you must take some action to renew interest in what you provide—more new product or service development.

If you expand to new markets, however, you can extend the life cycle of existing products or services by selling to customers who have not bought from you in the past. If your sales and support teams do their job right, you will create a whole new set of loyal customers, who will buy all your products or services, both existing and new, for life. Said another way, the investment in expansion tends to have a better long-term return.

Another distinguishing impact on volume relates to seasonality. If your business is affected by seasonality, you have a difficult time producing consistent financial results throughout the year. Many U.S. companies have a great fourth calendar quarter, then scrounge and scrape to pay the overhead in the first quarter. Volume peaks and valleys are different in different parts of the world.

If you sell skiing equipment, your big selling months may be November through February in the United States. If you expand into Chile, Argentina, or New Zealand, you add the months of May through August to your peak volume periods.

If you sell products and services to the government, fiscal years are different for different countries. The United States is on an October–September year, whereas Japan is on an April–March year. If you sell in the United States and Japan, your bottom line gets twice the impact of your salespeople helping those bureaucrats spend that unused budget.

Cost

Volume and revenue are not the only lines on the profit and loss statement that can have a favorable impact on the bottom line. Cost of goods and services is often an equally important consideration. Expanding your business geographically can have a favorable impact on costs.

The potential volume increases mentioned here should allow you to absorb your sunk costs, that is, development costs and fixed overhead, over a larger volume and thus decrease overhead as a percentage of revenue. Increased volume should also provide your vendors with more volume. Vendors should then pass their savings on to you as better pricing. Both actions yield better profit performance.

As in the volume discussion, though, there are some more subtle advantages at the cost of goods sold line on your profit and loss.

If you sell products that include electronic parts, for example, the chances are good that you buy components in Japan. If you have a presence in that market, you will be much closer to your vendors and have a much better understanding of the dynamics of their business. Being there is significantly different from traveling there. You can negotiate better prices, terms, and conditions if your people are constantly with the vendor.

If your products are high in labor content, it might make more sense to manufacture them somewhere other than the United States, somewhere with a lower labor rate. Many countries even offer tax incentives, low-interest capital loans, and training grants to companies that create manufacturing operations within their borders.

As you think about expansion, then, don't limit your scope to sales. You can have a procurement office in Japan or a manufacturing plant in Mexico without selling in either place. And, in many cases, that is enough. Costs will be positively impacted by doing that alone. Certainly, a deeper involvement in the local community, with sales and manufacturing and procurement, will have a more significant impact on the bottom line.

Don't get too starry-eyed about all this. As we will see in Chapter 6, preparing products and services for international consumption is not free. It takes money and effort to provide the right products and services for any given market. So you must balance that investment against any cost savings you might get from the concepts that have been expressed here.

Global Customer Support

In many businesses, the best prospect for revenue, and profit, is the large customer, the Fortune 500 account. That list includes a wide diversity of companies who have at least one thing in common: They all have international operations.

During your sales process with one of those companies, you will be told that you must support its branch office in Botswana in order to get the U.S. business. Let's hope this will not be the first time you have heard of Botswana. You will get a request like this, and you need to be prepared with an answer. If you do your homework correctly, you will be prepared.

In some companies with a more developed international strategy, customer requests or opportunities for specific orders often dictate the priority of market development. It is very possible that your entry into the world of global business will start with a requirement to support a specific customer.

Competition

As much as you like to think you control your own destiny, competition may force you to make a decision to expand. If your business falls behind competition in volume, you will ultimately lose position. If you don't support that Fortune 500 customer, the competition will. If you don't become the lowest-cost producer, you will not succeed for very long.

Keep an eye on competition. They are certainly looking at you.

HOW DO I BEGIN?

A blank sheet of paper can be the most difficult point at which to start a project. It is always a good idea to spend a little time organizing your thoughts so that you have at least one or two marks on that paper. Try to get preliminary answers to a few basic questions:

- Where?
- When?
- What?

Where?

The question of Where? can be approached from many different directions. Spending a lot of time thinking about the direction from which your inspiration will come is less fruitful than preparing for your reaction to the inspiration.

The answer to Where? may come from that customer who wants support in Botswana. It is, of course, unlikely that the support is required in such a remote location. It is possible, though, that the customer wants product in Canada or England. Those countries are a much easier location from which to start your international adventure.

If, however, you still have a blank sheet of paper, where do you begin? How about picking the largest market opportunity? That's fairly easy to determine. Just look at population as a measure of market opportunity. At least it's a start.

What are the most populous countries in the world? You have only 186 countries from which to choose. I'll bet you can name the first two. That's right—the People's Republic of China and India. The United States is next. The rest may be a surprise to you. Here is the list of the seven largest countries, ranked by population:

1.	People's Republic of China	1,169.6 million
2.	India	886.3
3.	United States	254.5
4.	Indonesia	195.7
5.	Brazil	158.2
6.	Russia	149.5
7.	Japan	124.4

Don't be surprised if you know very little about any of these countries except the United States. Except for the United States and Japan, the international trading traditions of these countries are in a stage of development that may make them unsuitable for a first-time entry into international business.

Many American companies make their international debuts in Europe. The international organization known as the European Community (EC) is made up of 12 member countries that are very used to trading with U.S. companies. Much of our heritage in the United States comes from Europe. Communications to and from Europe are easy.

You can choose to start somewhere that is close to your home office. Mexico and Canada are close to the United States. And we now have the benefit of the North American Free Trade Agreement (NAFTA).

You can begin with some country with which you may be familiar. Maybe you speak French or German or Spanish.

The point is made: Start to focus your thinking on some location from which you may want to initiate your international operations. Remember, we haven't spent any money yet for research. The information necessary to start your thinking is available in this book and at any public library.

When?

The question of When? is easier to answer because you already know when not to expand. You don't expand when you don't have the money, the resources, or the management bandwidth to handle the challenges you will face. As we go through the planning process, we will spend more time discussing the impact of expansion on resources. Other factors, however, can dictate the appropriate time to expand.

There can be great value in being first in a market.

Certainly, developing a market for a product or service involves risk. Being first may establish a leadership position that is easier to defend. The first fast-food franchise in Japan—McDonald's—has been wildly successful, and no one has been able to wrest the number one position from McDonald's.

All products and services have life cycles. As a product or service approaches the end of its life cycle in a particular market, that cycle may be extended through expansion into other markets. In the IT world, some markets develop a need for applications after other markets have already moved on to the next technology. Today, PCs based on the 386 processor are perfectly acceptable in some Latin American markets because they are being used as stand-alone word processors, whereas 486 PCs are required for the more developed network applications of Europe and the United States.

A word of caution here: Don't look on international markets, particularly the less-developed markets, as a dumping ground for old products. Buyers there are smarter than that. This has been tried before.

What?

What? may also be an easy question to answer if you have a narrow product or service offering—you sell what you have to offer. If you have a very broad range, however, you may want to pick and chose the right products or services for a specific market. It will almost certainly not be your whole range of offerings.

As you develop your thinking on products, be prepared to make changes. The cookie-cutter approach seldom works. For example, U.S. automobile manufacturers are very quick to point out how closed the Japanese market is to foreign imports. They were less quick, however, to provide a car with a steering wheel on the right-hand side.

Your products may be very suitable for a foreign market in the same way they are in the United States. There may be some necessary modifications, however, often driven by language requirements. The manuals may need to be translated into the local language. And the power supply may need to be changed to accept 220-volt supplies.

The What? may not be as straightforward as you may have thought.

WHERE SHOULD I LOOK FOR HELP IN UNDERSTANDING WHAT IS INVOLVED?

As you will see in Chapter 5, research is a critical element in your plan for expansion. Most research costs money, but you are in the very early stages of developing your plans. You are just kicking tires and not yet spending a lot of money. So, where can you turn for help?

First, you can keep reading this book. You will find a lot of ideas that will help you focus your efforts on a plan that has a good chance for success.

Next, explore sources of information that are free or inexpensive and readily available. For example, the U.S. Department of Commerce has many different sources of help for you. Each country with which American companies trade has a specialist in Washington who tracks the developments in that country. You can look in the Appendix for further details. The Department of Commerce also has hundreds of publications that can help. One that is particularly useful is available on CD-ROM. It is called the *National Trade Data Bank*. Just call your local district or regional office (the number is in the phone book) and ask for help.

The Central Intelligence Agency (CIA) publishes a book called *The World Factbook*. This book has all kinds of useful information about any country in the world. It lists all the countries, their population, form of government and political system, geography, along with economic data. You will find this a very useful source. Contact:

Superintendent of Documents
U.S. Government Printing Office
Washington, DC 20402–9325
Telephone 202–783–3238

The public library in your city is a good source of information. Call the research desk and ask some questions. You will find them to be quite helpful.

All countries with which the United States has diplomatic relations has some representation in Washington, DC, most as an embassy. Many countries have consulates in many different cities around the country. If you have a particular country in mind, contact the commercial officer at the embassy or consulate, and start asking questions.

Talk to people in your industry—your customers, your suppliers, your competitors. You will be amazed at how ready and willing some people are to help.

Finally, as you get a little more serious about your tire kicking, get the help of an outside expert. These consultants can help you brainstorm and test your ideas before you spend a lot of money on research. They can help you plan your research effort to get the most bang for the buck. They can help shape a strategy before you get too far along with your plans. The right consultant can provide services that are extremely valuable throughout your planning and execution cycle.

How Do I Apply Technology to the Process?

No, there is no magic button you push that is going to give you all the answers you want. In fact, at this stage of your planning, technology can't help a lot. You need to start with a few of your own ideas, focus on a few areas of inquiry, and put an overall structure around the plan. Build a straw man. Then, test it; criticize it; tear it down and build it back up. This will get you started down the right path.

There are a few technologies that will help you here. For a reasonable charge, most on-line services allow their users to access their research database. CompuServe, Prodigy, and America On-Line offer this service. There are other databases that you can subscribe to, such as Lexis and Nexis, if you want to do some legal research.

Now you have a few ideas that will take you from that blank sheet of paper to a sheet that has some marks on it. Apply your own understanding of your business to the project. Then, using the sources listed above, go and get some information about some countries that are of interest to you. Try the acid test: Does it make any sense to pursue international expansion? If so, proceed step by step.

In the next chapter, we discuss the elements of a business plan. We offer some suggestions on how to organize your thoughts further and how to line up your resources to dig deeper into the opportunities and challenges.

4

Internalizing the Decision

The early 1980s were the first of the boom years for the PC industry. Literally hundreds of companies were making IBM-compatible PCs, companies with names like Eagle, Hyperion, Columbia, and Corona. You haven't heard of them? Hmmmm . . .

Meanwhile, European consumers and entrepreneurs were watching this phenomenon, this PC explosion, with great interest. They had the vision; they saw the potential of the PC. They wanted the product.

For those companies that had a good product, the biggest problem in 1983 was product availability. The demand far outstripped the supply. Every PC made by a credible vendor was sold immediately. Compaq was one of these companies. As the international person at Compaq, I got telephone calls, I got telexes, I got checks, all from dealers and users who wanted to buy a Compaq PC overseas.

Many of the companies mentioned above also got those calls. They chose to take advantage of an opportunity to expand their business. Many went to Europe to gain a foothold before their competitors could. They would start with a distributor. Soon, they would find that that distributor was not very good. They would cancel that one and move on to the next. Then, they would add a few more channels. That didn't work very well, so they opened a sales office. After a short while, they fired the branch manager and hired another one. He moved the office closer to his home.

There was extremely limited supply. There was no technical support. There was confusion. There was frustration. There was no plan. As a student of history, I am reminded of Napoleon's march to Moscow. Among his other mistakes, Napoleon outran his supply lines. It was the beginning of the end for him. And, for the same reason, 1983 was the beginning of the end for many PC companies.

Other companies, like Compaq, chose a different tack. The industry was new. There were lessons to be learned. There were supply constraints. In 1983, Compaq chose to focus only on the dealer channel in the United States. Later, when there was more product availability, more money, more management bandwidth, we put together a plan to enter Europe. Today, international business accounts for about 50% of Compaq's $10 billion in revenue. For the first half of 1994, it was the number one provider of PCs in the world.

In any business enterprise, there are many opportunities presented, many choices to be made. If you snap at those opportunities carelessly, without considering the consequences, you will ultimately pay the price.

How can you avoid jumping at the wrong opportunity or the wrong approach to the right opportunity? How can you get all the resources in your organization moving in the same direction to arrive at the right decision? Cause the organization to accept the decision to globalize and to make it the personal commitment of each individual in the company. Consider the internal implications of the changes required for global expansion.

WHO NEEDS A PLAN?

One option, of course, is to move ahead without a formal plan. If you work for a young, fast-moving company, you don't have the time to create a formal, written plan. If you work for an older, more mature company, you have been successful so far. Why waste time on a plan? Before you jump in without a plan, however, consider some of the benefits of planning:

1. Planning encourages systematic thinking ahead by the management team. Since international expansion is new to you, you will be better served to approach it systematically.

2. Planning leads to better coordination of corporate resources. International expansion will be a major effort for your company. Maximum leverage of your limited resources is critical to overall success.

3. Planning leads to the development of standards of measurement. This will provide you a way to keep score, to see if the effort is successful.

4. Planning causes your company to refine its objectives for expansion and revisit its policies to test their applicability to the international effort.

5. Thinking about the unexpected in advance makes you better prepared to manage the surprises when they arise.

6. Team members have a stronger bond of participation among themselves, and their organizations are much more inclined to support the effort to which their boss has committed them.

Developing the world's great markets is a walk in the park compared to the problems typically encountered in the internal decision process that leads to a truly international company. You, the expert, are the internal salesperson. Don't get too carried away by what lies ahead. Remember Matthew 13:57, where we read, "A prophet is not without honor, except in his own country, and in his own house." Good luck! You'll need it!

In the summer of 1983, I took a Compaq portable computer to Europe. This was the first step in the development of an international strategy for the company. I wanted to talk to people in Europe to gain an understanding of the market requirements. The best way to describe the product to such an audience is to demonstrate it.

The power sources in European countries range from 220 to 240 VAC, while in the United States the source is 110 volts. Today, portability in a computer presumes that it will work on any power source around the world. That was not the case in 1983. Special arrangements had to be made. I went to the engineers and asked what was required to change the power supply to work on European power sources. They said that we simply had to cut a jumper and change the fan. We did just that, and I was on my way. Easy!

When I arrived in London for the first demonstration, I plugged the machine into the wall, turned it on, and watched it smoke and sparkle. The power source in the

United Kingdom is 240 volts, the high end of the power source range in Europe. This was clearly outside the range of tolerance designed into this power supply.

When I returned to the United States, I told the designer of the power supply what had happened. He scratched his chin and recalled having the same problem at his previous company. I asked if he had done anything different in the design of this power supply. "No," he said.

This engineer was not stupid. He was not a bad person. He had no intention of designing a bad product. He simply did not know that the products he designed needed to comprehend different voltage requirements. You will experience many incidents like this throughout the development of your globalization plan. You need to be prepared for them. You need to make your company internalize the decision to expand the business internationally. That is the internal sales job.

COMMUNICATE BROADLY

Your company is full of intelligent, well-intentioned, motivated people. If you let them know what you want, they will respond with remarkably innovative ideas. I have found that the best way to create awareness of the requirements for international business is to communicate broadly throughout the company.

As you develop an understanding of the requirements for international business, let people know. You will find that they are very interested and can be very helpful in offering ideas. For example, as you develop the product requirements, tell the engineers and the product marketing people about them. Let them know that it is important to translate documents into 14 different languages; that the next personal computer they design needs a Southern Hemisphere monitor; that many countries have extensive government agencies that regulate the smallest detail of products imported into their jurisdiction.

Once the people involved understand the requirements and needs, you will be flooded with innovative and creative ideas on how to address each one.

There are many ways to communicate the message, to preach the gospel. For example, at Compaq, I had several signs made up that said: "Think International." I put these signs in the offices of key people around the company and in the design labs and hallways. You would be amazed at the amount of interest these signs created.

Use the company newsletter. I remember one article that had a particularly positive impact; it began, "How many power cords do you need to run a computer in Europe? The answer is 6." This created a broad awareness that something was happening in the company that was different, and interested people began to learn more about it.

Technology can really help here. Use E-mail to broadcast new information about what is going on outside the United States. The more people know about what is going on and what is required, the more interested they will get.

BE PREPARED FOR CHANGES

As you work through all the details of the "international plan," you will identify processes in your company that must change. Making your business global is very much a reengineering of your internal business processes. Those processes will become more complex, and so you need to consider the principles of reengineering about which you have heard so much.

1. Because the changes required to make your business global reach to every corner of the company, organize your work around results, not tasks. The goal, for example, is to design a worldwide product. Create a team that includes engineering, marketing, sales, and service to plan for the achievement of that goal.

2. Allow decision points at the location where the work is performed. Allow the manager in the local country, for example, to run the business there. Don't require home office approval on every decision.

3. Work in parallel as opposed to sequentially. As you go through your research, for example, don't wait for the distribution section to be completed before you start the pricing research. After you have completed all the research, you can integrate the results.

4. Capture data only once when it is first created. For example, create a database of all your research so that everyone can access the information when and where it is needed.

5. Let technology help you establish controls in your processes. Put the mechanisms for accountability and security into the information-processing system you use. For example, as you develop your distribution strategy, restrict the access to that portion of the database that has the names of key contacts in the distributors' organizations. Limit access to your product strategy to the engineers and marketing people who need to know it.

6. Make the people who do the work use the process. As the writers develop the documentation, for example, make them use the same word processing system the translator will use.

7. Treat geographical resources as if they were all available anywhere in the world. Be creative in the use of technology here. Try to use video conferencing to have "virtual" meetings. Create a forum such as E-mail through which your team can communicate.

This is not the place for an exhaustive discourse on business process reengineering (BPR). But, as you begin your planning process, you need to consider these principles. They will have an impact on what you do and how you do it. If you are interested in learning more about BPR, the Appendix contains information on reference materials.

SOME IDEAS TO MAKE THIS WORK

You have scratched the surface of the opportunity. You have some idea of the internal job to be done. You are about to cause fundamental change in your company. Just before you jump into this with both feet, let me offer a few hints on how to make this work more smoothly.

1. Get top management commitment. If you are top management, make sure you communicate that commitment throughout the organization.

2. Develop a clear vision early in the process. Without it, you will waste time and money and may never succeed.

3. Establish cross-functional teams of people who are willing and able to get the job done.

4. Pay attention to internal politics. You are dealing with people and organizations and how they work. Be sensitive.

5. Communicate broadly and frequently.

6. Don't start in Botswana—you probably won't succeed. Start with a place or an opportunity that will work.

7. Take reasonable risks.

8. Bring lots of money. This isn't cheap.

9. Don't give up. You will be frustrated; you will be angry; you will meet resistance. In the end, however, it will be worth it.

THE PLAN

As you proceed, then, with the development of your plan, there are two approaches you may choose to take. They are not inconsistent with one another, and you will probably end up with a mixture of both.

The Decisions

The first approach is to spell out the decisions you will have to make to create a global company. You have already looked at the big picture, and you understand some of the implications involved. Here is what will follow:

- Get the organization to agree to go ahead.
- Decide which markets to enter.
- Decide how to enter each market.

- Decide what you will do when you enter. What products will you sell? Which programs will you implement?

- Decide the right organization for each market.

The Process Flow

The other approach is to identify the various parts of a business plan that will allow you and your team to address all the key issues involved in creating a global enterprise. Those issues fall into six categories:

1. Research—defining the opportunity

2. Finding the path to success

3. Product strategy

4. Distribution strategy

5. Promotion strategy

6. Financial planning

In the next chapter, we discuss research. The planning process involves a series of decisions. Some are based on the internal environment; some are heavily influenced by external factors. Research should be the foundation on which you will base almost every externally influenced decision.

5

Research, Research, Research!

How many times have we seen companies spend large amounts of money developing very sophisticated products or programs to address markets about which they know little or nothing! They are then surprised when they fail in their attempts to enter the market.

Although a business model may have worked quite well in the United States, the cookie cutter is seldom, if ever, successful. For example, manufacturing cars with a steering wheel on the left-hand side works well in the United States but not very well in England.

In this chapter, we look at sources of market research information and a down-to-earth approach to gathering the necessary information to proceed with the project.

THE RESEARCH PLAN

Remember, as you develop your research plan, that you are trying to find the answers to these fundamental issues:

- Decide which markets to enter.

- Decide how to enter each market.

- Decide on what you will do when you enter.

- Decide on the right organization for each market.

Establish a plan that describes what you want to know, how much you are willing to pay for it, and when you want it. Then, you can begin to look for the answers. Remember, research is like anything else—you want it yesterday. But you get to choose only two things from a list of three—good, quick, and cheap. The results can be:

1. Good and quick, but not cheap

2. Cheap and good, but not quick

3. Quick and cheap, but not good

Prepare your ideas and concepts so that you will know what to expect at the end of the research project. I suggest you consider some of the following issues:

- Which markets are most attractive for what you have to offer?
  Rank them in order of importance and chance for success.

- What are the requirements to enter that market?
  Rank them in order of importance.

- What are the product or service requirements for a specific market?

  Dig in and understand them fully.

- How does the distribution system work?

- What is the pricing structure for your industry in the market?

  Look at retail pricing, dealer pricing, and margin structures.

- What promotional opportunities exist?
  Trade shows
  Press activity
  Advertising

- What are the U.S. export rules for your product?

- What are the local import rules?

- What is the potential impact of trade initiatives like NAFTA, GATT, and LAIA?

- What is the ultimate path to success for your company in that market?

If you organize your thoughts in such a way as to define the ultimate deliverable, you will have a much better chance of getting what you need to proceed down the path to success. Without a road map, though, you will probably spend too much money, take too long to get the answers, and not end up with what you thought you wanted.

AN EXAMPLE OF THE PROCESS

Let's look at an example of how to gather the required information when almost nothing is obvious and first impressions are almost always wrong.

While working for Compaq Computer Corporation, I began seriously investigating the Japanese personal computer market in 1988. There was very little information available to the casual observer to indicate how a non-Japanese PC vendor could be successful there. Clearly, Japanese PC buyers weren't waiting for another vendor to provide them with product. There were plenty of PCs available from known Japanese companies.

The Japanese market was dominated by a series of closed, proprietary implementations of the Intel microprocessor and Microsoft operating system combination that we knew in the rest of the world. NEC had more than 50% market share. The distribution channels were unlike those of any other market in the world. The products were fundamentally different. (Most of the differences were driven by language.) The distribution of market share of the industry differed from that of any other market. The top five PC vendors provided 90% of the PC consumption. (As a point of reference, the top five U.S. vendors accounted for only 40% of the total market consumption.) Customer demands for service and support were overwhelming.

I think you get the point: The market was one of the most arcane in the world. Although I had been working in Japan for 10 years, in the minicomputer business, I had little understanding of the complexities of the PC industry there.

In addition to being complex and hard to understand, the Japanese PC market was, and is, the second-largest single market in the world, second only to the United States. This simply meant that there was an opportunity that could not be overlooked.

Networking

As I was traveling to various places in Southeast Asia to work on other, easier markets, I would stop in Japan. The first thing I did was to talk to people I knew from the past and people who were well known in the PC industry. There was little cost involved since I was traveling anyway and the conversations were casual discussions about industry issues.

This process could be described as an extended exercise in networking. I would talk to one person about a specific subject and get suggestions from him or her about other people to contact. In fairly short order, I was able to get in touch with a lot of people and to get answers to some fundamental questions:

- How big is the market?
- Who are the market share leaders?
- Who are the major software vendors?
- Who are the key dealers and distributors?

These answers, however, revealed no clear path to success. Most people told me that the only way to be successful in Japan was to build an NEC clone and sell it for 30% less. This didn't look like a good long-term strategy for Compaq. There was no leverage of the things that made Compaq successful: compatibility with the industry standard, brand awareness, and channel loyalty.

At about this same time, another U.S. PC vendor was trying to enter the Japanese market. It announced a plan to build a machine that was compatible with the NEC PC 9800 and with the industry standard that was prevalent in the rest of the world. Apparently, that company had heeded the same advice I had been given. In addition, it had a U.S. Trade Representative (USTR) official at the press conference at which the company announced its intentions.

The market response was interesting and predictable. The audience asked why the company was building a clone of the NEC PC. Why not build something else? NEC can provide plenty of their products. The market didn't need any foreign clones of a Japanese machine. (There was one authorized clone—Seiko-Epson—in the market already.) Further, there was skepticism as to how one machine could be compatible with two standards that were incompatible at the hardware level.

The reaction to the USTR was predictable. This was during the time that Carla Hills, the U.S. Trade Representative for the Bush Administration, was flying over to Japan every month trying to get trade concessions. This was not a happy time for United States–Japan relations. Tension was high. At the launch, the Japanese press reacted badly to having the USTR there. The message the media got was all negative and was not focused on the real purpose for the conference.

This was not a good example of proper utilization of research. These negative reactions to the plan could easily have been predicted if the company had invested in the right level of research. Needless to say, that company has not been successful in Japan.

The answer, then, was not lying on the surface. More digging was required.

Secondary Research

The next thing I did to continue the research in Japan was to do some secondary research. In Japan, as in other markets around the world, there are many market research sources that are not very expensive.

- The governments of most countries, including the United States, have extensive research capabilities. Some services are free and some cost money. Check out the U.S. Department of Commerce (USDOC) for research services. You can find some information about the USDOC services in the Appendix.

- Don't forget the public library. The amount of information available there never ceases to amaze me. With the more sophisticated research tools available at the library, you can get some very good information fairly quickly. Call the research desk of the downtown branch of your library.

- Most industries have trade associations. These associations can refer you to their offices in Washington or in many foreign capitals. They have a lot of good market data and have extensive contacts they can introduce you to. Remember, these are trade associations and they usually have their own agenda. But, if you accept the bias, the information can be useful.

- Research firms have a wide variety of information for sales to their clients. Many routine reports for these firms will give you valuable information about your market potential. These research firms are in the business of selling information. It is best to confirm the value of their product. It is a good idea to deal with a company you know. If you don't know any, ask your associates for some suggestions.

As you gather this research, be aware of language difficulties. In many cases, there is good, reliable information available in English. This can usually be obtained from international research companies such as A.C. Nielson and Company, International Data Corporation, or Data-quest. In some of the more esoteric markets, English-language research may not always be available, and you may have to rely on local-language data.

When dealing with a research company in a foreign country, be prepared for some frustration and surprises. One company I dealt with in Japan provided me with both. This was a company I had dealt with in other markets, and so I was sure the information they gave me would be good. Wrong assumption!

I found out that you must be very specific in articulating the assignment. I asked the president of this research firm to prepare a presentation about the strategies of various PC vendors in Japan. The audience for the presentation was to be a senior executive of Compaq.

When we arrived for the meeting, we found that the presenter had prepared a few paragraphs on each vendor. The information presented was, at best, superficial. He had the volume produced by each company, a range of suggested retail prices for their products, and a list of some of their dealers. This was clearly not very strategic and was, indeed, very frustrating.

In addition to being frustrated about the poor communication, I was surprised at the lack of insight into the data. As I looked at the market numbers, I noticed that each year there was a prediction that the next year in the period covered was going to show dramatic growth. And yet, as I looked back over the actual volume of years past, I saw no growth. This was the proverbial "hockey stick" that you see in many plans.

On digging further, I found that the source of information for this presentation was a Japanese government agency. This organization, made up of many, but not all, of the PC vendors in Japan, provided monthly reports of market share and market volume. The agency got its data from the vendors and simply accumulated the information; they applied no judgment to the data.

This information, while looking pretty on the charts, was useless. It showed no insight into what had happened in the past or what would happen in the future. That was the chief source of my frustration and surprise.

A few final words of advice about secondary research are in order here:

- Prepare a budget, and know what you are willing to spend.

- Check out the companies you engage. Get references.

- Don't rely on just one company's information.

- Don't assume that, if a company is good in one country, it is good in another. Dig into the local capabilities.

- Ask about the company's sources.

- Build a relationship with the local researchers—the people—whether they work for an international company or a local company. They will be great sources of information.

- Be willing to spend some money to have foreign-language research translated. It may be your best source of information.

Technology Helps Out

Today, technology provides us with a very good source of information that wasn't readily available to me when I was exploring the market in Japan. Public information services have been around for a long time. Some actually started in the late 1960s, but they were available to only a few subscribers who had a lot of money to spend. Today, millions of PCs and modems are installed around the world. Any one of these can access a remarkable variety of information that is helpful in research.

There are several hundred on-line services available worldwide. They put a huge treasury of information at your fingertips. After you have used a few of these services, you'll never want to go back to the public library. Resist that temptation. Keep going to the library, but use the on-line services as another research tool.

These services are not free. The entry fee may be small but, as you go through a project, you can rack up some fairly hefty bills. Almost always, however, these costs are smaller than an airplane ticket and a hotel bill.

Some examples of on-line research services areas are as follows:

- Dialog is a research service with many databases that cover books and periodicals, allowing you to search multiple sources of information simultaneously.

- Nexis, Lexis, and Mexis are three services from Mead Data that cover news, the legal profession, and the medical profession, respectively.

- The Dow Jones News/Retrieval Service is directed at the business community, covering publications such as *The Wall Street Journal* and *BusinessWeek*.

- Knowledge Index is a service of CompuServe that has 27 sections, each containing one or more databases. The information ranges from Arts and Literature to Business and Industry to a full text database of *USA Today*.

Another possibility for research information from the on-line service is the forum. Services like CompuServe, Prodigy, and America On-line are general-purpose services. They offer everything from the latest news to shopping services to travel information. They also provide a link through which people can talk to one another.

Within these services, you will find a variety of highly focused forums. There may be a Japan forum, a European forum, or a PC technology forum. Through these forums, people talk to one another about specific topics. They can be a great source of tips or leads that can then be followed up with more traditional research techniques.

The Outsider

Getting assistance from an outside consulting firm can be very helpful in any or all stages of a research project. Depending on the firm, consultants can help in preparing and formulating the research plan, and they can make execution a lot easier and more efficient. I found the outside approach very helpful in the Japan project.

We engaged a consulting firm to help us get a lot of in-depth information about the Japanese PC market very quickly. There was a sense of urgency in our project. We were convinced that the market was changing very rapidly. We had a window of opportunity that could close if we didn't respond expeditiously. This meant that we needed a firm that had extensive local capabilities and that could get good results quickly. This meant, of course, that they were not cheap.

Before you take this step, understand what your criteria are for selecting the right firm. In our case, we wanted a firm that had local Japanese analysts who could get to the source very quickly. This may not be a requirement for you. You may be completely satisfied with a United States–based firm that has some good understanding of how United States–based companies do business in a particular area of the world. The point is to make this a conscious decision, not an accident.

The consulting firm helped us put together, and execute, a fairly extensive research plan. It involved procurement of some local secondary research as well as some very specific primary research. It included one-on-one interviews with PC users and dealers. We had a very detailed plan to address the independent software vendors (ISVs).

When the project was over, we had the information—and the understanding—that was necessary to proceed. We were able to convince ourselves, and the board of directors, that we had a good understanding of the market requirements and that we had identified a clear path to success for Compaq in Japan.

Research should be considered one of the basic building blocks for creating a global enterprise. It is fundamental to success. We hear all the time about how markets are closed to outsiders. Japan is a frequent target of this criticism. But experience has shown, time and time again, that, if you provide a product or service that meets a market need, it will sell.

Use your research resources well. Focus on the answers you need to make the important decisions about your expansion plans. Use it to understand the real market requirements.

In the next chapter, we discuss your product and how it can be made attractive to foreign buyers and distribution channels.

6

The Product Plan

This is a test. Have you ever seen one of these?

How about this?

Surely you recognize this.

If you are going to sell electrical products in Japan or the United Kingdom or Italy, you will soon recognize the first as the Japan Industrial Standard (JIS) mark, the second as the British Standards mark, and the third as the Comitato Elettrotecnico Italiano mark. Your products will need to be modified to meet these and many other standards, and the labels will need to be modified to include these marks.

The product you sell must be good, or your company would not exist. You will find, however, if you have not already done so, that the sale of a successful product in the United States does not always translate directly into successful sales internationally. The world is not the same all over.

In Quebec, Canada, the law requires the words printed on retail packaging to be in French. In England, drivers drive on the left-hand side of the road. In Western Australia, the electricity provided to the plug is 270 volts. Television sets used in the United States don't work in South Africa. It is illegal to chew gum in Singapore. The Chevrolet Nova, translated into Spanish as *no va*, means, "It doesn't go."

In this chapter, we examine methods of finding real product requirements and how to identify, engineer, and implement them.

Traditionally, global companies have had to make a choice between two different product development approaches:

1. For each market, create customized products that respond to specific requirements in that market.

2. Provide the same product to all markets to get maximum leverage of manufacturing resources and brand awareness.

The chosen path depends heavily on the product. There is not much room for customization of soybeans. On the other hand, English language books don't sell very well in Argentina. In reality, the best answer may lie in using both approaches to get the benefits of each. Let me explain by way of example.

GLOBALIZATION VERSUS CUSTOMIZATION

When the IBM PC was introduced in 1981, it was directed primarily at the U.S. market. It was an English language keyboard. The power supply was 110 volts. The plug was the standard three-pronged U.S. plug. The documentation and software were in English.

The Open Industry Standard

There was, however, one very strange thing about this machine. It was based on an *open architecture*. That was something that had never happened before. The microprocessor—the central processing unit (CPU)—was made by Intel, not IBM. The operating system was written by Microsoft, not IBM. And, most important, any company could write an application or build an add-in board that would work on this machine. All the developer had to do was read the book that came with the machine to get the required specifications.

A product like the IBM PC could not stay restricted to the United States very long. Soon, the machine was available in Europe with a 220-volt power supply, translated documentation and software, and a keyboard that supported many local languages. In very short order, the architecture of the IBM PC became the standard of the new PC industry. Soon, there were millions of PCs that were compatible with this standard. And these machines were available in almost every country around the world.

The basic product was global. The CPU, the memory subsystem, the video subsystem, the I/O bus, and the plastic and sheet metal housing were the same worldwide. The only things that had to be changed to get a "local" product were the keyboard, the software, and the documentation. These localized pieces accounted for less than 10% of the total cost of the machine.

The Closed Proprietary Model

Contrast this scenario with the situation in the Japanese PC market. The industry standard that was so quickly adapted in every other market in the world could not manage the Japanese language.

The Japanese language is made up of three alphabets: *katakana, hiragana,* and *kanji.* The first two are phonetic, and the last is ideographic. It is the kanji characters that cause the problem.

The IBM PC was based on one 8-bit byte of code as the basic word. A byte is equal to 2 to the power of 8 (2^8), which equals 256. In Western, nonideographic languages, all characters can be depicted in a standardized code—ASCII code—of 256 unique characters. In Japanese, there are roughly 6000 kanji characters in the everyday language of business.

The industry standard machine would not handle the kanji characters. The CPU was too slow. The monitor supported only an 8 × 8 character cell while kanji characters need at least 16 × 16—preferably 24 × 24—to be adequately represented. The mass storage medium—the 360-Kbyte diskette—was not big enough to hold the dictionary for Japanese, let alone anything else like an application program or data.

NEC was the pioneer in the Japanese PC industry. In 1981, it introduced a PC—the PC 9800—that could manage the Japanese language very well. There was a hardware solution to the management of the kanji characters. The keyboard looked very much like a Western-language keyboard. It had a Roman character set as well as a *kana* character set. Kana is a term used to describe both katakana and hiragana characters. There was a piece of software called a front-end processor (FEP) that managed the conversion from Roman or kana homonyms to the kanji ideograms. This machine worked very well in Japan. It didn't work anywhere else.

With that description of the globalized versus the customized products, let's look at the PC market situation today. Most markets outside Japan embrace the open industry standard product. The penetration of the PC market ranges from well over 50% in the United States to around 40% in Europe. The two top manufacturers of PCs in the world, IBM and Compaq, make more than 6 million PCs a year.

NEC is not a factor in any other market in the world. They have chosen a "customized" approach to product development. They continue to enhance their 9800 standard in Japan. But the market is limited. In 1993, Japanese buyers consumed 2.3 million PCs. Assuming NEC had 50% market share, it sold 1.15 million 9800 PCs. In the rest of the world, which accounts for more than 95%

of the total PC consumption, NEC sold less than 500,000 units.

Since the 500,000 units sold by NEC outside Japan are fundamentally different from those sold in Japan, there is little leverage to be gained from manufacturing or marketing. NEC cannot be the least-cost manufacturer (6 million vs. 500,000) and, since the names are different (PC 9800 vs. PowerMate), NEC gets no brand leverage. NEC, which has such a great reputation in Japan, cannot be counted as successful in the PC market outside Japan.

I don't want to mislead you into believing that these are the only reasons that the Japanese PC market is different and that NEC has been unsuccessful in the PC business outside Japan. These are not the only reasons. Further, this is a historical perspective. The PC market in Japan—and in the rest of the world—is changing dramatically and rapidly. And so the situation described here is also changing.

I am using this story to illustrate the different approaches to product development. Please don't draw any other conclusions from these facts. I will describe this situation in more detail through the rest of the book to illustrate different points. Here I am pointing out the impact of two different strategies that led, in part, to completely different results.

You have to decide which approach is best for your product. Make this a conscious decision based on the results of the research you conduct. In most cases, some product modification is in order.

WHY MODIFY THE PRODUCT?

There are as many reasons to modify a product for sale internationally as there are products and companies and countries. Here are a few that you should consider in making your decisions regarding your products.

1. *The law of the land* I am sure you will not be surprised to learn that most governments feel the urge to touch the lives of their citizens with lots of different regulations regarding all facets of products, ranging from safety to the environment.

Any buyer of electrical products in the United States has seen the UL seal. Consumers who purchase packaged food products see a label listing the nutritional value of the contents. Automobile manufacturers are very familiar with government regulations.

2. *Stopped at the border* A few years ago, it was against the law to import a fully assembled PC into India. You could, on the other hand, import parts and subassemblies. In Australia, a PC manufacturer got credit for adding local value to the landed cost of a PC. These credits were used to determine how much that vendor could sell the government.

And, of course, when the United States gets involved in sword rattling with Japan, all sorts of tariffs go up. A few years ago, there was a 160% duty on the import into the United States of colored flat-panel displays for PCs. Manufacturers like IBM, Apple, and Compaq simply moved the manufacture of affected products offshore. The jobs went with the manufacturing.

The way your products are classified by the various import authorities has a huge impact on the duty rate you will pay. Get competent expert advice on this issue because it is incredibly complex. And, not surprisingly, the rules change frequently.

3. *The invisible walls* Some years ago, when the market for computerized telephone exchanges (PBXs) was expanding, U.S. companies like Rolm built a great business making these devices. Japan provided a huge market opportunity. However, in order to import a PBX into Japan, the manufacturer had to have it approved by a variety of government agencies.

The documentation for the PBX had to be translated into Japanese. This was a huge undertaking. In addition, the manufacturer had to submit reliability data for the PBX, describing the mean time between failure of each individual component.

When Spain entered the European Community, there was no domestic computer industry. And, as a member of the EC, Spain could impose no tariffs on imported products. But imported products had to be "homologated." *Homologation* is an approval process that products must go through. It costs money and time and discourages the free import of goods.

These are examples of nontariff barriers to market entry that could suggest product modification.

4. Regional trade agreements   The United States just entered into a free trade agreement with Mexico to complement the one we already have with Canada. This agreement is known as the North American Free Trade Agreement, or NAFTA.

Twelve European countries have joined together in what is known as the European Community (EC). The goal is to create a common market among the various nations. The EC is a bit behind schedule on reaching the goal.

The Association of Southeast Asian Nations (ASEAN) is made up of six countries and is devoted to creating economic growth in the region.

The Latin American Integration Association (LAIA) has 11 members, who want to develop a more open regional trade.

There are many other such associations; they are listed

in the Appendix. Each association exists so that its members will have a competitive edge in the region over nonmembers. This is almost always done through the imposition of duties.

The best way to avoid the negative implications of being an outsider is to manufacture in the region. Many companies, for example, manufacture products in Europe so that they are not at a cost disadvantage among their European competitors.

5. What's the other guy doing?   Lee Iacocca was a very vocal critic of the closed Japanese automobile market. And yet his company, Chrysler Corporation, did not make a car with a steering wheel on the right-hand side. All the Japanese competitors did. When Chrysler changed its products and moved the steering wheel to the right side of the car, its market share in Japan increased.

Any consumer product in France, for example, that did not use the French language on packaging and in documentation would be at a competitive disadvantage in relation to a product that offered this feature.

In each case, your market research will identify the features you need to have to compete and may also turn up some others that will put you at a competitive advantage.

6. When in Rome . . .   Accommodating cultural differences may be the most difficult reason for modification that you will face because it may be the hardest to understand. This is sometimes easy to see in the way some countries adapt technology. For example, in Japan, it is very unusual to see a high-level manager using a PC. It requires typing, and managers don't type; secretaries do. And, yet, managers readily use fax machines because faxing is the quickest way to transmit their handwritten notes.

Culture may have a more serious impact on your programs, which will be covered in Chapter 7, and in your advertising strategy, which will be covered in Chapter 8.

7. *Economic development*   The economy of the market in which you are interested must be able to support your product, both economically and technically. Somalia, with an annual per capita gross domestic product (GDP) of around $200, is probably not a good market for luxury goods like jewelry or perfume, whereas Switzerland is.

Selling sophisticated wide area network (WAN) systems, a hot item in the United States, would probably not yield a lot of return in Ecuador. The phone system there just won't support the technology yet. In Singapore, on the other hand, the government is committed to have, by 1996, every home connected to a fiber-optics network.

8. *Who makes the decision?*   There is no place in the world where purchasing and distribution patterns have more effect on products and programs than in Japan.

In the United States, if a fairly high-priced product—say, a disk drive in a computer—breaks, the user takes it to a shop and gets it fixed. If it is a business application, a service technician comes out and fixes it. In Japan, if a computer breaks, the retail consumer will act similarly to the U.S. buyer. He will take it into a shop for repair. A business application is a bit different.

Yes, the technician will go and fix the disk. But, in addition, the manufacturer must go out to the customer's site, apologize for the disk crash, and describe to the customer what the engineering and manufacturing organizations have done to prevent a similar failure in the future.

If you don't have the level of quality in your products

to respond profitably to this kind of customer demand, don't sell them in Japan.

The distribution systems will have a severe impact on your business, most importantly on your cost of sales. We will discuss this in more detail in Chapter 7. However, those differences may cause you to rethink your program offering.

Have you ever walked into a car dealer's showroom? They are usually large places with lots of cars on display. Salespeople hang around waiting for a customer to walk into their clutches. In Tokyo, one of the most densely populated areas in the world, there are no large car showrooms—there isn't enough room. Salespeople go out to visit customers door-to-door.

9. Where in the world are you? I have already alluded to a change that may be required because of geography —the monitor in a computer or a TV set. Because of the different properties in the magnetic fields of the North Pole and the South Pole, the magnets in a cathode-ray tube need to be adjusted differently, depending on whether you're in the Northern or Southern Hemisphere.

Climate can have an impact on products. On my first trip to India, I noticed that all PCs that had a hard-disk drive were enclosed in a strange-looking box. My host explained that the heat, dust, and humidity in Bombay did not allow the smooth operation of hard disks—they just wouldn't work in an open, unprotected environment. The boxes contained air-conditioning devices that cooled and filtered the air so that the disk could work.

Your product may not need modification. Many things, like steel, paper, and shop towels, don't need localization. You can count yourself lucky and move on to the other issues that will demand consideration—distribution, communication, and organization, just to pick a few.

If you are not prepared to make modifications, for whatever reason, you may go to foreign markets and find customers who are willing to buy your product as is. This can work very well but usually for short periods of time. At Compaq, when we entered a new market, we usually offered unmodified product initially. The target customers were usually branch offices of U.S. multinational companies. Later, as we learned more about the market requirements, we made modifications and sold product to local companies as well.

The point here is to alert you to the potential issue of product change. And the message is, "Be prepared." Get ready to respond if changes are required.

How Do You Modify a Product?

Let's assume that you are one of the unlucky companies that has to modify your product. How should you do that? How can you approach the issue?

You have identified the market requirements through your research. You understand what is required of products in the selected market. There are many factors, of course, that affect the right decisions regarding product modifications in your company. You need to consider as many factors as are necessary to reach the right conclusion. Here I just want to raise some questions in your mind so that you will consider some things you may not have comprehended in your initial thoughts.

Consider:

- Who will make the modifications?
  Internal people
  External contractors

- What is the extent of the modification?
  Adaptation
  Invention

Inside your company, you have your own ways and means to change products. In the classical large organization, that process usually involves a brand or product manager, an engineering team, and a manufacturing team. If your process works, use it in making the modifications necessary for international markets. If it doesn't, go fix it and make it work. Then, use the working process to implement the required changes.

What if you don't have the internal expertise to make the required changes? What if your product is application software, say, an accounting package? You want to sell in France. Do you have someone who knows the French language and the French accounting system? If not, you need to find some external resources to help do the work. You can hire the resources or you can contract for them. When you use outside resources, beware of the not-invented-here (NIH) syndrome. We all know engineers who are never happy with a product or a feature that was designed or developed by someone else.

The nature of the modifications—whether it's a change or an actual invention—will depend on two issues. One is driven by external forces, the market requirements. The other deals with internal issues, cost. Let's look at each.

You have some product that you want to sell. So, start there. That is your strength, and so you want to leverage it as much as possible. Create a new retail package for Spain that is in Spanish. Or create a European box that has Spanish, French, German, Italian, and English messages. Throw in a French manual at the end of the manufacturing line for the widget you make. Put a three-mode diskette drive in the PCs you are selling in Japan so that the computer can read the NEC diskette format. These are changes.

You may find, however, a unique situation or demand in some foreign market that calls for the invention of a new product. In Japan, executives are crazy about golf. There are many golfers and not very many golf courses. Getting a tee time at the local club may take an entire morning of dialing and redialing the pro shop number. Now, golfers can buy a device that uses answering machine technology and an autodialer to do this for them.

The internal factors may impact what modifications you make or what inventions you create. You will find, however, fairly early in your international life, that changes are usually very expensive. If you begin your modifications by taking finished product off the end of the manufacturing line, you may waste a lot of money. If the volume is small and your margins are large, you can afford this, at least for a while. The nature of your product may require that you proceed in this manner.

Consider, however, another approach. Let's take computer software as the example. If you know that you will sell your product in many different countries where different languages are spoken, comprehend that fact in your initial product design. Don't bury the messages that the user sees in the code of the program. Break the messages out into separate, easily translated text files that are called by the application when needed. In this way, you need support only one version of source code.

If you know you are going to sell product in countries that have ideographic languages—Japanese, Chinese, Korean—put double-byte character support in your product when you create it. It is very expensive, and maybe impossible, to go back and insert this feature.

This is one of the most difficult concepts to get your organization to accept. As you develop your product plans, insist on the inclusion of those features that are required by your international markets. That is the cheapest and the fastest way to get "global" products.

WHERE DO YOU MAKE THE CHANGES?

I cannot overemphasize the importance of comprehending the requirements as early in the development process as possible. A final issue that you might want to consider is where you make the changes to the product. There are a few determining factors here: volume, product complexity, and extent of modifications.

If the changes are minor or if they require local knowledge—language, for example—it may be best to make them in the local country. In a computer manufacturing operation, stopping the line that makes 10,000 units a day to isolate the five units a week that need a Greek keyboard is probably not the right answer.

If, on the other hand, the modifications are extensive, requiring manufacturing and engineering support and perhaps affecting the quality of the finished product, it may be better to make them back in the factory. If you make power systems for large production plants, changing a 110-volt turbine engine to a 220-volt engine may not be able to be done in the field.

Another consideration for the Where? may be local governmental rules. Some of the incentives offered or penalties imposed may affect the way you do business. If the local government either requires or encourages local value to be added to the finished product, the localization effort may be best applied locally. Duty rates may be lower for the import of kits than for fully assembled products.

In this chapter, we have looked at a variety of product issues that may have a serious impact on your international business. I have not intended to cover all the answers exhaustively. Products are very specific to a company for many reasons, some technical, some financial, and some emotional. You need to make the right product decisions. The issues we have considered here will help you think about the factors that will affect those decisions.

Now that you have the perfect product for the selected market, how do you sell it? In the next chapter, we discuss the distribution issue and look at a variety of ways to sell and support products on a worldwide basis.

7

So, How Do We Sell This Stuff?

Cracking a distribution channel in a foreign country can be an interesting challenge. When I started kicking tires for Compaq in Japan, I saw a lot of interest in the product. The channels, however, were not willing to sell and promote Compaq computers openly for fear of what their current vendors would do to them.

After two years of visiting, talking, and demonstrating, I saw little progress. I was a *gaijin,* a foreigner, and, as good as my personal relationships with the dealers were, they were not willing to risk the wrath of the vendors who accounted for the vast majority of their business. One dealer, who was partially owned by his sole vendor, was willing to sell our products to customers who asked for them.

After we hired the president of the Japanese subsidiary, things picked up a bit. We actually signed up dealers. However, there was still reluctance on the part of the very large dealers to work openly with us. One principal in one of the major companies would meet with the Compaq CEO when he visited, but only in a hotel room away from his office. Other dealers would accept shipment of Compaq products, but only in warehouses far distant from their normal place of business.

It was only after the team at the local Compaq subsidiary created the demand for the product that these dealers came out of the closet and openly supported Compaq. This was after almost two years of concentrated effort by the local team. An interesting challenge, indeed!

In this chapter, we look at the various alternatives available to you in selling your product. Of all the decisions you will make about your international expansion, the distribution decisions will be the most far-reaching. It is very difficult to implement a fundamental change in your strategy and, at the same time, keep the buyer and the channel happy and confident.

ESTABLISH YOUR GOALS UP FRONT

Because there are so many different ways to address the distribution issue, you must first get a clear understanding of your goals. Prepare a list of things you want from your chosen distribution strategy. Your list might include:

- Demand generation
- An effective sales force
- Sales volume
- A financial model that generates profit

- Local inventory

- Local billing in local currency

- An efficient support mechanism

- Control of your own destiny

There may be other goals that are peculiar to your business. Make sure you identify and prioritize those goals. As you look at the distribution alternatives, you will find that there are tradeoffs. You need to know your priorities to intelligently select the right options. As we discuss the various distribution alternatives, I will describe some of the pros and cons of the alternatives relative to these goals.

DISTRIBUTION ALTERNATIVES

Now that you have established and prioritized your goals, let's look at some distribution alternatives. In considering these choices, think about how one or more of them might best fit your business and your goals. You will find that combinations sometimes work very well. Further, your strategy will most certainly evolve over time. For example, you may start with a direct export model and end up with a direct investment model.

The distribution chain flows from the manufacturer's backdoor to the hands of the ultimate consumer, as shown in the flowchart, Figure 7.1. In between, there are many steps. The closer you stay to your backdoor, the lower your risk and the lower your reward. The farther you move down the chain, provided you do it right, the higher the risk and the higher the potential reward.

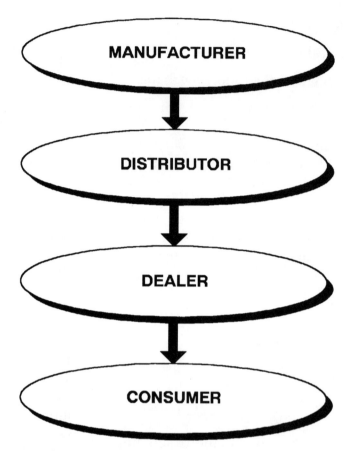

Figure 7.1 The distribution chain.

Direct Export

The easiest, quickest way to get into international business is to export product directly from the United States to a foreign destination. For example, a customer sends you a purchase order and an irrevocable letter of credit for the purchase price of the product drawn on a U.S. bank (this will be discussed in more detail in Chapter 10). You send him the product. End of transaction. Of course, nothing is really quite that simple, but let's expand on that scenario and fill in a few details.

In 1973, Datapoint Corporation, a high-flying minicomputer company of the 1970s, entered into an exclusive distribution agreement with a subsidiary of TRW called TRW Datacom. The plan was very simple. TRW would enter orders on Datapoint. TRW would pick up the product at the Datapoint factory. TRW would pay for the product. That was all Datapoint had to worry about. TRW would do everything else. It would appoint subdistributors around the world. It would develop the market and create demand. It would take care of all export licensing.

This was a great deal for Datapoint. International business accounted for more than 60% (it eventually moved to 50%) of Datapoint's revenue. It was cash business. The volume was relatively high and very predictable. The bad news for Datapoint was that it had no control of its destiny outside the United States. It had no control over local pricing or the quality of local support and no control over market development. As a result, it did not optimize its market position internationally.

It was a great deal for TRW, which got an entire product development and manufacturing operation for no capital investment. It had a complete product line to sell worldwide. And it could run the business the way it wanted, thus maximizing its profits. The bad news for TRW was that it had no control over its product costs and no control over product availability. The only way TRW could maintain or increase profit was to increase prices. That resulted in a limited market share against more price-savvy competitors.

This arrangement worked quite well for the boom years of the minicomputer business—the 1970s. Margins were high, the market was growing, and there was a lot of demand. It fell apart, however, when the market stopped growing and margins started to shrink. Then the parties involved turned on each other, and the deal ultimately fell apart.

Datapoint bought back its international distribution rights and bought TRW's equity in the distributors around the world. Datapoint paid entirely too much money. The timing of the purchase couldn't have been worse. As a result of this buyback (and many other internal and external factors), Datapoint is no longer a factor in the market.

There are many other flavors of direct export. You can move up the distribution chain and take on more responsibilities while still working exclusively from the United States. For example, you can choose to manage the export of products to a distributor you have signed up in Singapore. You can choose to be paid in Singapore dollars. You can give the distributor 60-day open credit terms. You can consign local inventory to the distributor.

Assuming that you execute the rest of the plan right, direct export usually provides some attractive advantages:

1. Quicker market entry

2. Positive cash flow

3. Lower risk

4. Lower investment

The disadvantages are:

1. Lower control

2. Less direct understanding of the market

3. Lower profit margins

Direct Investment

This form of distribution is at the other end of the spectrum. In this case, you start a wholly owned subsidiary operation or build a manufacturing plant in the targeted country or create a direct sales force. This is the approach, for example, that IBM took in most markets as it moved around the world.

The direct investment approach to distribution provides:

1. *A very high level of control*   You have made the investments; now, you get to manage the business your way.

2. *The best market understanding*   It is your employees who are there, managing the business, working against the competition, and dealing with the consumers.

3. *The highest margin*   You have cut out all the go-betweens and get to pocket their profits.

Since we all know there is no free lunch, we need to consider some of the negatives:

1. *Big investment in money and time*   You need to hire people, select the distribution partners, and analyze the market requirements; that takes money and time.

2. *High risk*   If you hire the wrong people, chose the wrong dealers, or misread the requirements, you are in the ditch.

3. *Administrative infrastructure*   You need to do all the things necessary to support that remote branch office or factory; that involves basic changes to your entire administrative operation.

This approach tends to work better with large, well-capitalized companies that can afford relatively high investments in exchange for relatively high returns. The advantages are so compelling that they are willing to take the risk, make the investments, and withstand the changes to get at the return and the control.

These two approaches to distribution—direct export and direct investment—can be used in the same company over time. A case in point is Compaq.

One of the primary goals at Compaq was to retain control and ultimately establish a wholly owned subsidiary. Another primary goal was to move quickly to take advantage of market opportunities. These goals—to maintain control and to move quickly—seem to conflict with one another. In fact, they complemented each other. Here's how it worked.

The real effort to develop an international business for Compaq began in 1984 in Europe. We began with two subsidiaries, Germany and the United Kingdom. The German office in Munich served as European headquarters. In the headquarters operation, we added infrastructure to support more expansion in the region.

There were other markets in Europe in which we didn't want to miss opportunities—places like Spain, Belgium, and Italy. Those were countries in which we eventually wanted subsidiaries, but not in 1984. We found dealers who could work remotely, with support from the Munich headquarters. We told them that we planned ultimately to start a local subsidiary. But, in the meantime, they could distribute our products. When the subsidiary was finally started and distribution expanded, they would have the advantage of being already established as Compaq dealers.

The same approach was taken in areas like Australia, Southeast Asia, China, Japan, and Latin America. It worked very well. Compaq got earlier entry into these markets, and the dealers had a degree of exclusivity for a period of time.

Joint Venture

Another approach is to find a partner to help. Joining one company with another to plan and execute a distribution strategy can take many forms. Whatever the form or whatever the purpose, I will generally refer to this activity as a joint venture (JV). Some of the more popular forms of JVs for distribution purposes are:

- Joint ownership in a separate company

- Joint equity investments in existing companies

- Licensing arrangements

Usually, these arrangements involve something in addition to distribution—contract manufacturing or joint product development, for example. Joint ventures usually work because of leverage. Both partners—and there may be more than two—have something the other wants. Fuji had access to the Japanese market, and Xerox had copiers to sell. They got together and formed Fuji Xerox. Pharmaceutical companies tend to use this tool to get into various markets around the world.

In some cases, JVs are dictated because of government requirements. If this happens, it is usually in one of the developing countries. There often is a government policy to grow local understanding of a particular industry or a need to protect local currency from erosion in value against hard currencies. The government wants foreign investment with local participation.

These arrangements can be very formal, with extensive contracts and agreements to cover all sorts of contingencies. Or they can be fairly loose, with companies agreeing to cooperate in the respective, complementary product developments. This works very well in an open industry like the PC industry.

In a JV, as I said earlier, the key advantage is leverage. You put together one of these JVs on the premise that synergy exists and will be realized. As you might expect, this isn't free. The key disadvantage is that JVs are very difficult to manage over the long term. Imagine, in addition to blending two or more national cultures, that you have to throw in two or more corporate cultures! That's a real challenge. Because of this, many JVs are short-lived.

WHAT TO EXPECT

Regardless of which approach you take, you should set your level of expectation correctly and make sure that everyone involved understands. Said another way, you, the U.S. company or headquarters, will contribute something to the effort. The distributor, the local subsidiary, or the JV partner will contribute something. And you will share some things. Here is an example of how that division of effort could be structured:

What the U.S. Company Contributes

- *Product supply:* This is the basis for the arrangement in the first place. You provide the products, enough to meet demand. The products have the right level of quality and the right set of features to meet local requirements.

- *Exclusivity:* If you use a distributor, it will want a quid pro quo for its investment in the market. This usually takes the form of an exclusive contract for a period of time.

- *Margins or commissions:*   You have to pay the local staff for the job done. In a buy/sell distribution arrangement, that payment to the distributor is its margin, the difference between distributor cost and resale price. In the case of a representative, agent, or even your own salespeople, the payment is a commission.

- *Support for the local effort:*   These people are your representatives in the market. They will need training. They need constant and effective communications. They need motivation. They need to see you regularly.

What the Local Company Contributes

- *Local market knowledge:*   Who is better positioned to tell you what is going on in a market than your local team. It doesn't matter if they work for you or for your distributor. They know the market best. They know what the economy is doing. They know what the competition is doing. They know what the product requirements are. In many cases, they can help with product development or localization. Let them know you expect this knowledge and then ask them for it.

- *Local administration:*   This can be as simple as managing the telephone and answering inquiries and as complex as managing local inventory and accounts receivable.

- *Demand creation:*   Yes, there will be spillover awareness from your home country into the local market.

But the real demand creation takes place locally, through advertising, event marketing, press activity.

- *Forecasts:*   The local company must give you a sales forecast so that you know what parts to buy and what products to build. A note of caution here: Make sure you are very clear and precise in detailing what is required by way of forecasts. Your view of a forecast may be very different from the distributor's or local manager's view. Forecasting is an alien concept in some countries, particularly where the economy is supply-driven, not demand-driven.

- *Translation support:*   When your documentation or packaging needs translation, ask your local team to help. They know the language best. Even if you employ a professional translation company, and one that is highly recommended, get your local team to help with the glossary and proofreading.

What Should Be Shared

- *Risk and reward:*   Distribution is all about sharing risks. If you want to pass on all the risk to the channel, be prepared to pass on the reward as well. If you are willing to take some risk, take some of the reward. For example, impose quotas on distributors to keep their exclusivity but allow for inventory returns if your product doesn't sell.

TIERS OF DISTRIBUTION

You need to spend some time thinking about how many tiers of distribution you need and are able and willing to support. For example, if you make very complex, expensive products, a direct sales force—a no-tiered distribution model—may be best. The sales cycle is long and involves high levels of top management support. And the margins support a very high cost of sales. If, on the other hand, you sell high-volume, very inexpensive products, indirect distribution may be appropriate.

Some products in some markets may require more than one tier of distribution. For example, to get a consumer electronics product into a shop in Akihabara in Tokyo, you probably need to go through a distributor, then a wholesaler, then a jobber, then the dealer and, ultimately, to the consumer. The shops are so tied into this method of distribution that you will probably never be able to get to them more directly. If that is the case, you need to make sure your products have plenty of margin so that everyone can get a piece of the pie.

Remember, though, economic times are changing. Nothing is forever. And so, around the world today, there is a trend toward more efficient distribution mechanisms. If a tier of distribution doesn't add real value to the proposition, it will not last very long. But you need to recognize that different markets have different concepts of what real value is.

THE CONTRACT

You probably have a lawyer who works on your contracts. If you don't, get one before you start this adventure. And, by the way, don't even think about doing all this on a handshake. You will ultimately pay dearly for that bit of fantasy.

My intent here is not to write a contract for you—let your lawyers do that—but, rather, to alert you to a few issues peculiar to international transactions that should be considered.

There are export and import laws in every country around the world. You should state in the contract that compliance with these laws is a condition for continuance of the agreement. We will discuss some of the export rules later in this chapter.

The financial implications of international business deserve some consideration. Pay attention to credit terms. Letters of credit are a frequently used tool in many international transactions. Currency fluctuations may adversely impact your ability to make a profit or to sell product against local competition. For a further discussion of these issues, see Chapter 10.

Look into the implications of applicable law. You may not want to have your rights and obligations under your contract governed by the laws of Togo. And, yet, the application of U.S. law may not be appropriate either. The same may be said for jurisdiction and venue. These issues need detailed professional legal advice.

Define the territory correctly. Make sure you have agreement on which countries are covered, and then get the correct names into the contract. And make sure the distributor cannot reexport to other territories unless you agree. Such reexport will not only lead to export law problems (see the next section), but will also infringe on the franchise of your distributors—or future distributors—in that territory.

The other issues that should be covered in the contract are similar to those issues faced in conducting domestic business. You are already familiar with these, and so there is no need to go into them here.

THE RULES OF THE TRADE

The U.S. government, like any other government, likes to dabble in trade regulations. The basic law governing export of goods from the United States is called the Export Administration Act. It, and the 100-foot-high stack of paper that the bureaucrats have managed to generate under its aegis, will confuse and befuddle you. Under this law, and all the regulations, you may need to get a license from the government to export your products. The law covers not only the export of goods and information from the United States but also the reexport from the original country to which you shipped your product to some other country.

The U.S. laws, because they do not have an indexing scheme that allows the limits established under the regulations to change automatically with changes in technology, cause constant headaches for exports of high-tech products. Technology is constantly bumping up against the limits imposed by the regulations. This has been further complicated by the fact that the United States was a member of the now-defunct COCOM, the Coordinating Committee for Export Controls. The founding purpose of COCOM was to regulate the export of high-tech products to Communist countries.

Not very long ago—five years or so—a PC manufacturer had to get an individual validated license to export a 386-based PC to the People's Republic of China or Russia although anyone could walk into any computer store in any country in the world and easily buy one of these computers without restriction.

Fortunately, with all the political changes in the world, the rules are changing. Computer manufacturers are springing up all over the world. Now there are much higher limits on the speed and power of high-tech products that used to be so strictly controlled. COCOM is gone. The laws are recognizing the realities of open world trade. The government controls exports in a much more practical way.

Even with all the changes in the laws, we still have a

complete trade embargo on some countries. A recent list of embargoed countries includes Cuba, Iran, Iraq, Libya, North Korea, and Syria. Check with the USDOC for the current list.

Technology has helped this whole area of export licensing dramatically. A company that wanted to export products used to have to fill out a form and mail it to the right export control office in Washington, where it would sit on someone's desk for days without any action. It would take anywhere from two to six weeks to get a routine export license granted. I have had licenses take months to get approval. By exception, you could speed this process up and ask for special processing of your request. But it was really the exception and not the rule and was not allowed very often.

Today, most export licenses are filed and granted electronically. You make application to the Department of Commerce for this facility. Once you are approved, you can use the PC on your desk to file the application. The whole process now takes only a day or two for a routine license.

Product Classification

One important aspect of the regulations relates to the classification of products. This is a method of applying different rules to different products, depending on the trade policy of the government at the time the regulation was written. Trying to understand this area is like a trip through the looking glass. If the U.S. Customs people classify your product in one way, you may freely export it. But, if it falls into another class, you may need an individual export license that takes time and administrative effort to get. Classification of goods is not only important for export but will also have a severe impact on the duty rates you pay when you import to the destination. Get expert help and you will save time, money, and a lot of grief.

There are special rules regarding the control of weapons—nuclear, biological, and chemical. There are also special considerations regarding licensing of high-tech products to countries like India and Pakistan that have not signed the Nuclear Nonproliferation Treaty.

Antiboycott Regulations

As a result of the past conflicts in the Middle East, we have antiboycott regulations. As a matter of national policy, we are opposed to boycotts or restrictive trade practices imposed on countries that are friendly to us. U.S. companies are prohibited from participating in any way in such activity. This applies anywhere in the world, but it comes up most frequently in doing business in the Middle East.

This is not as simple as it seems. For example, if you are presented with a request, verbally or in writing, not to use El Al Airline to ship your oil tools to the Middle East oil fields, you cannot comply; you cannot tell the requesting party that you will or won't comply with the request—you can say nothing—and you must report it to the Office of Antiboycott Compliance.

Bribery and Corruption

Another area of regulation that is peculiar to international trade is the Foreign Corrupt Practices Act (FCPA). This law grew out of the scandals of the early 1970s, when American companies were bribing foreign government officials in order to get business. We can argue for hours about imposing our moral standards on other countries. It doesn't matter that our foreign competitors are not encumbered with such rules. We are. And you need to understand these requirements fully. Breaking the law can result in criminal penalties.

There are some circumstances in which you can offer foreign officials, like customs officials, a tip or gratuity for getting goods through customs. But these are very limited and need to be understood well before you venture into that gray area of the law.

LOCAL RULES

The impact of foreign laws on your business may be more important than you expect. For example, some countries have strict laws that protect local companies. This is particularly prevalent in Latin America. These laws make it very difficult, if not impossible, to cancel a contract with a distributor or a dealer. If you do cancel, it may cost a lot of money to compensate the local company for its expenses in setting up, its inventory, the value of the goodwill it established for you, and loss of its potential future profits. Make sure you understand these rules, and decide if you are willing to follow them. If not, don't distribute in that country.

Trading Alliances

There are many trade alliances among various nations around the world. Examples are the North American Free Trade Agreement, the Association of Southeast Asian Nations (ASEAN), and the European Community (EC). I have included a list of them in the Appendix. Most of these alliances arose from a desire to provide a competitive advantage to the member nations against nonmember nations in the area of the world covered by the alliance. This is most often done through favorable duty rates.

However, as we learned during the debate in Congress over NAFTA, the relationships often involve much more than just duty rates. They deal with environmental issues, banking and currency control, and even political policies.

Here in the United States, we are quite used to restricting dealers to assigned territories. We do this through requirements for support and service. In Europe, in the EC (sometimes called the Common Market), you can't restrict a dealer this way. Dealers have the right to sell product anywhere in the Common Market. This kind of situation may have an impact on your distribution strategy for Europe.

Get Help

The rules for export and import are confusing. Get professional help in understanding their impact on your business. You will find that this is money well spent. You will be surprised at how much time and effort will be saved if you get this part of your strategy absolutely correct. Then, you will be in a good position to execute properly.

8

*Image Is
Everything!*

*Nos esforzamos más. Nous faisons plus
pour vous satisfaire. Wir geben uns mehr Mühe. Wij doen
nòg meer ons best. Fazemos mais por você. Hooikaika oi aku
makou. Mi jobban igyekszünk. Tunajitahidi sana. Ymdrechwn
yn galetach.* We try harder.

When Avis communicates its message to consumers
in 140 countries around the world, it doesn't always use
an exact translation of the English words; sometimes
that just doesn't work. The correct local words may
translate back into English as "We put in more effort";
or "Our goal is your satisfaction." But, in all cases, the
message is consistent: Avis is committed to providing
the quality and service the customer expects.

In this chapter, we focus on the communications strategy. We look at the various tools available for communicating the right message to buyers and prospects. Some

are obvious, like advertising, press relations, and event marketing. And some are not, like documentation, dealer sales incentive plans, internal communications, and the name of the product. We discuss how you can communicate a consistent message around the world regardless of the tool you use.

How Communications Work

Planning is key to a successful communications effort. You can make a mistake in product planning and correct it internally before the product ever gets to the public. Even if the mistake makes it to the finished product, you may be able to sell around it. Communications, on the other hand, is a very public exercise from the beginning. It is also an exercise in numbers—you want to communicate to as many people as possible within the limits of your resources. So, sending the wrong message can take lots of time and money to correct.

To help lay the foundation for a great communications strategy, first, you should consider the elements of communications. In his book *Principles of Marketing,* Prentice Hall, 1986, Philip Kotler offers us a good model, as adapted in Figure 8.1. This model will help you visualize how you might want to design your strategy. Start with the response you want to elicit from people receiving the communication. You want them to buy. Before they buy, however, they must be aware of your offering, they must understand it, they must like it, and they must decide to buy it. The desired response to a communication may be very different from country to country because of the stage of development of a specific market.

For example, a buyer in the United States may know all about your company and your product. The response

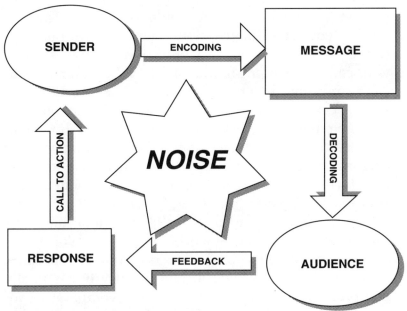

Figure 8.1 The communications process.

you want from that buyer is the decision to buy. This will call for a particular combination of message and media. If, on the other hand, you have just entered a new market, you might direct your communications at creating awareness of your brand in the mind of the receiver. This suggests a different message.

In order to create an effective strategy, you must determine a way to measure response and create the appropriate feedback to your target audience. For example, test your brand awareness in a market before and after a campaign. If you are new in the market, there is no need to test before the effort—your awareness is probably close to zero. But test afterward.

The target audience for the communications may also be different from country to country. Your market research will show you the right audience in a specific market. If you want to sell major appliances in Japan, your target is the housewife. She makes the decision. In the United States, the decision is much more collaborative between husband and wife, which suggests that your communication should target the husband as well.

The message is, of course, critical. Selling PCs in a sophisticated market might lead you to focus on your implementation of local bus graphics and how that speeds up video response. If, on the other hand, you are creating a strategy for a newly developed market, you may focus more on educating the receiver about what a PC can do to make work easier, faster, or better.

The message is the most difficult element of communications to manage on a worldwide basis. Words and concepts do not always translate exactly. In some cases, a message is appropriate in one country but is totally inappropriate in another. For example, comparative advertising is common in the United States but is illegal in Europe.

Whatever your message, it should be simple, easy to understand, and consistent. If not, you will waste a lot of money.

Finally, you must recognize that things will go wrong. There will be a lot of noise or static in the process. For example, look at your local newspaper or listen to the radio during rush hour. Everyone is trying to sell you something. Your communications must get above the noise to be heard. If you don't comprehend this element in your plan, your message will become distorted and misunderstood by the receiver. Local competitors are very good at creating noise around a foreign company's message in the home market.

These, then, are the elements of communications. As you work through your strategy, you need to consider all of them.

Now, let's look at various types of communications and how to manage them.

ADVERTISING

The creative process in advertising is very specific to a relationship between the agency and you, the client. Without dwelling on that process, let me make a few points. You must make sure your agency understands that its work product must address markets other than just the United States. If the agency knows this up front, you can minimize wasted effort in the design phase.

The real issue regarding advertising, and to a lesser extent press relations, is the management of the agencies. You have two choices that are inconsistent with one another: centralize or decentralize. Both approaches have advantages and disadvantages.

Regardless of which approach you take, you should establish some minimal guidelines for all advertising. You should require:

- The same "look," that is, similar layouts, with similar areas devoted to words and to graphic elements

- Consistent treatment of the logo

- Consistent color schemes

- Centralized review of all advertising before it is run

This list of "requirements" will still give the local team lots of flexibility in what they do. At the same time, this minimal list will support either the centralized or the decentralized approach.

The Centralized Approach

The centralized approach gives you the most control over the message and your budget. You can find one agency that will give you worldwide coverage. There are several available. The agency will manage the creative development through a centralized program manager working with the creative people at their headquarters and at their local offices. The program manager will provide you with a media plan for each market. The agency can almost always provide you with one invoice that consolidates billings around the world.

The obvious benefit to this approach is control. The centralized model gives you the most consistent possible worldwide message. It gives you the tightest control over the budget, both for creative development and ad placement. It gives you the most influence over the artwork and wording of each ad. And it gives you a single point of contact for program management of your advertising effort.

The major disadvantage is that a consistent worldwide approach may conflict with local requirements. The content of an ad may be very different from market to market, depending on the stage of development of the market. Sometimes, the central staff may not understand the local market enough to guide you through this issue.

As an example, at Compaq, we were designing an ad to introduce the company to the markets in Southeast Asia. Compaq was founded in 1982, the year of the dog on the Chinese calendar. The concept was to draw on the good attributes of the dog—loyalty, friendliness, honesty, dedication to purpose—and to show how those attributes apply to Compaq as a company.

The agency in the United States agreed with me that this was a great idea. Very clever, very Chinese! Unfortunately, when we checked it with the agency in Hong Kong, we were told that the dog evoked many negative connotations in the Chinese mind and that using that image would be a disaster.

Another serious disadvantage of the centralized, one-agency approach is that there are very few, if any, agencies that have offices in every market around the world. For example, very few U.S. agencies have effective offices in Japan. The Japanese agency Densu dominates the market. Many U.S. firms try to collaborate with local firms, with varying degrees of success.

Many companies, teamed with good agencies, have successfully used this centralized approach and have overcome all the negatives.

The Decentralized Approach

When you want to have maximum flexibility at the local level, go for the decentralized approach. This allows the most appropriate response to local conditions. The agencies are local. They live and breathe in that market and know it best. Because advertising is so creative, a centralized bureaucracy may get in the way of creating the perfect ad for the target audience.

Two big disadvantages of the decentralized approach are ease of management and cost. If you are in only one market outside the United States, this isn't a problem. If, on the other hand, you sell in 60 markets around the world, you don't want to have 60 different agencies to manage. This leads to inconsistency in message and inflation in costs. The artwork is generated by different people, the media plans are prepared in different formats, and the communication about positioning to many agencies is very difficult.

The decentralized approach may work well if you are conducting business through a distributor. That relationship can be so good that you can manage all the disadvantages.

As you can see, there are options. You need to make the choice that is best for your situation. But, whichever

choice you make, there are a few things you should do
to get the most out of your advertising dollars.

- Pick an agency or agencies that meet your needs,
  not the other way around.

- Get all the agencies, or offices of the agency,
  involved early in the product development cycle.
  The creative people need to understand the product
  fully from concept and positioning through to the
  features, functions, and benefits.

- Have regular meetings—at least annually—with
  the worldwide team to communicate the goals and
  objectives of the company for the coming planning
  period.

- Enforce your guidelines to make sure the work
  complies.

- Listen to the local team, and be prepared to be
  flexible. It is not the same world all around the
  planet.

PRESS

There are a few things about press relations around the
world that are different from the U.S. model. You should
know them.

Managing the press in Europe is just as difficult as it
is in the United States. Journalists around the world are
driven by similar forces. They want good, interesting
stories to titillate their readers and make themselves famous; they're looking for the next Watergate story. Foreign press people are, to varying degrees, aggressive. In
short, the techniques you use to manage them in the
United States apply elsewhere.

In the United States, the press wants to remain very aloof and above reproach when it comes to dealing with industry. When you throw a press conference at your headquarters, the invited press from the United States expects to pay their own way. They don't want to be overly influenced by a free trip. The foreign press, on the other hand, expects a free ride—you pay their way.

In Japan, the press is organized into press clubs, roughly aligned with various sectors of industry and government. When you communicate with the press, you need to make sure you don't offend one club by going to another first. In this situation, a local press relations expert is absolutely necessary.

EVENT MARKETING

Another potentially effective way of delivering a message is through event marketing. An event can be anything from a simple executive breakfast, to which you invite a few key people to participate in an open discussion of a specific topic, to a trade show, which tens of thousands of people attend to see the latest and greatest products and services.

Picking the right event strategy can be confusing. There are endless ways to spend your money. Your challenge is to pick the most effective ones. Those choices will not be the same all over the world.

In markets that are in a fairly early stage of development, trade shows tend to work pretty well. The buyers in a particular industry, who generally have limited resources to go to events, like to go to an event that shows them the broadest possible range of offerings.

Large trade shows can be important to a company that is new to a market. If you are new in the computer business in Japan, the Business Show in May or the Data

Show in September provides excellent opportunities to address a large number of prospects. The problem with large trade shows is that, if you want to do it right, you will spend a lot of money. If you are to be a serious contender, you should expect that anyway.

For a little more help in trying to decide which shows to attend, call the U.S. Department of Commerce (see the Appendix for the phone number), and ask for some help. The Department of Commerce helps thousands of companies a year by sponsoring U.S. pavilions at many shows around the world. In addition, a partial list of trade shows around the world is included in the Appendix.

If you are trying to enter one of the more developed markets around the world, such as Europe, Australia, and Japan, try to run a seminar or an executive breakfast directed at a very specific set of prospects. The list of invitees might contain some of the key influential buyers of your class of product in that country.

When it began operations in the United Kingdom in 1984, Compaq did an excellent job of running a series of seminars targeted at a specific audience. For example, they ran a seminar, in partnership with Lotus Development Corporation, directed at bankers. The information communicated during the event told bankers how to operate their businesses more effectively using Compaq computers and Lotus 1-2-3.

Seminar selling can be very good in developing markets as well. The key challenges are: Get the right list of people to invite and, once you get them into a room, make sure they go away believing that their time was well spent.

DOCUMENTATION

Documentation—the materials you use to describe your product—says a lot about your company and your product. How often have you bought a consumer electronics product, opened the book, and laughed at the poorly translated user's guide? Imagine what buyers in France would think about your product if they had the same experience with your documentation!

You must surely have been told that today you can buy any number of software packages that translate English into a variety of languages. You just plug in the English and out comes the Japanese. Sound too good to be true? It is.

At Compaq, we had a very elaborate system for translating all sorts of documentation. Most of the documentation was developed internally by a staff of highly talented professionals. We also engaged two or three—the number changed from time to time—outside professional translation firms. Through a collaborative effort of these groups of people, we were able to get books translated fairly quickly and efficiently. And technology made it all easier and more efficient.

At Compaq, the technical writer is a key member of the product development team. As the product is developed, the writer develops the attendant documentation. This is done in English. As the first complete draft of a book is completed and reviewed internally, the word processing files are sent electronically to the translation company. Their translators begin the process of translation.

The tools available to translators are incredibly powerful and efficient. But, even with all the tools of the trade, good-quality translation requires a good professional translator—a real person. Unlike the old days, when paper was the medium for sending the words back and forth, technology has provided some very powerful tools to the translator. Since the only product a translator has to sell is time, that's what you pay for—the translator's time. So, the use of technology not only makes the work better, it makes it cheaper.

Most modern translation systems can use a variety of word processors and a variety of graphics packages. You need to decide which software to use and work with the translation firm to make sure they can use it. Once you pick the right software tools, stick with them. The word processing element of the system has a split screen. One window contains the English version of the book and the other the local language. The translator reads one language from one window and types the translation in the other window.

Another key element in translation systems today is a glossary of terms. Your company has words that describe what you do and what your products are. You use these words consistently in your communications to the U.S. market. This same level of consistency should be used in other markets as well. The glossary of translated words provides the tool to do this. The side benefit is that you don't have to retranslate the word each time it comes up in the text of the message. That saves money.

The principles that apply to the glossary of words can also be used with phrases. Once you pay for the translation of a phrase, the system should store that translation for future use. Then, as a new book is developed, the translator will do a software compare with books already translated. If there are matches, the work effort is minimized. This is not an automatic process yet, but it does save time and effort and provides consistency.

The writers, of course, have to cooperate in order to make these tools really effective. They have to use consistent terms and phrases. If one writer writes: "The quick brown fox ran through the field," another can't have the option to write: "Through the field ran the quick brown fox." That will require a new translation effort.

Now, back to the Compaq example. . . . As the drafts were completed, they were sent to the translation firms, who performed the project management task for the process. These files were very large, and the file transfers were tedious and full of frustrations. But they were far better than the alternative. The translators, usually located in the targeted country, would do the file compares, incorporate what was useful for the book in question, and translate the rest.

Through an iterative process of review by the local Compaq office, the translated version would be complete. The completed work then flowed into the publication process.

Documentation, like all forms of communication, may not be simply a good translation of the English words. Buyers in the target market may not understand the function of your product. Users in the United States may want detailed technical information because they already know how to use the basic product. That may be very different in Japan. There, you may have to spend more time explaining some more fundamental concepts about your product since that class of product may be new to the user.

As you develop documentation, think about this translation process. If you use more pictures and fewer words, you will have less to translate. The graphic element makes the documentation more interesting to the reader as well.

PRODUCT NAMES

The name of a product should say a lot about the product. It should support the product positioning. Not all names, however, are appropriate for all markets. We have already mentioned the Chevrolet Nova, translated into Spanish as *no va*, which means "no go."

Diet Coke is not available in some markets because it would have to be sold through a pharmacy. Coke Lite, which is not the same thing, is often sold instead. The Japanese drink called Pocari Sweat—they use those exact words—may not be a very big seller here.

When you pick your product names, try to make them "international." If that isn't possible, be prepared to use different names. Not only may some product names not make sense in other countries, they may not even be legally usable. There are people in this world who make a good living registering trademarks for famous, and not yet famous, products in various countries around the world. Once they own the local trademark registration, they just sit back and wait for the product to show up in their country, at which time they go to the manufacturer and offer to sell the name for a tidy sum of money.

Volumes have been written about communications. Here, I have offered some ideas for dealing with the peculiarities of international communications. The real point is to make sure that you comprehend the global nature of your business as early in the process as possible. The result will be better communications and less waste of precious resources.

In the next chapter, we discuss the value proposition, the ways you make your products more valuable to the prospective buyer.

9

The Value Proposition

     When Compaq entered the Japanese market in 1992, conventional wisdom provided very clear guidelines for pricing. Price the product at 20% below the comparably configured NEC product and hope it will sell.

This wisdom made a lot of sense. Personal computers in Japan, including NEC PCs, carried about a 30% price umbrella over similar products sold in non-Japanese markets. And so, pricing at 20% below the market price and allowing 8% for costs in getting the products from the United States to Japan still left two points of additional profit. Great idea!

A great idea that wouldn't work. History has provided us with many examples of companies that tried to compete with a dominant market leader by selling comparable products at a significantly lower price. Can you think of any company that has succeeded with this strategy over the long term? Yes, there are hundreds of companies that made a quick buck by getting under a price umbrella provided by the market leader. There are even some that lasted beyond the initial success. But I know of no company that became a major market force over the long term by pricing significantly below the dominant market leader.

One reason this strategy doesn't work is that the market leader always has the option of meeting or beating a lower price offered by a competitor. Usually, the market leader is a bigger company with deeper pockets. That means it can last longer in a price war.

Another reason this strategy doesn't work is that it says something very negative about your product. It says your product is less valuable than the leading product. If you say that, the buyer will ultimately believe you.

We took a different approach at Compaq. We knew our products were better than NEC's for many reasons. At the initial product launch, we priced our products at, or slightly above, the comparably configured local Japanese products, including NEC's. Compaq products were more powerful, were fully compatible with over 200 millions PCs installed around the world, could handle all the local language requirements, and had an incredibly high degree of quality. The pricing supported that image. The buyers quickly believed us.

This was the first step in a two-step strategy. I discuss the second step later in this chapter.

The value of a product or service is what the buyer thinks it is. As a vendor, you just need to help the buyer understand the value of your product. His opinion, if you do your job right, will coincide with yours, and you will make a profit on the sale.

In this chapter, we discuss the value proposition and

how you can influence what the buyer thinks of your product. We look at pricing, costs, and profits. We investigate pricing as a delivery mechanism of compensation for the distribution channels. We review the impact of the right strategy on the success of your venture.

PRICING

The price of a product is a key element in your marketing strategy. Many companies use price to position the product in the market. An effective pricing strategy can deliver profit to you and to your distribution channels. Like most other decisions you make, both internal and external factors affect your pricing strategy. Let's look inside first.

Internal Issues

As with every part of the planning process, your goals and objectives for the pricing strategy must be clear. If you want maximum profit, price your products high. If you are looking for market share, price them low. If you want to establish a good distribution and support relationship with distributors, give them a high margin. If you will support your products with your own staff, lower the distributors' margin. These are factors that will influence your conscious decision to price your products in a certain way.

Your internal cost structure will surely influence your pricing strategy. You will probably want to sell your product at a price that is higher than your cost. However, that may not be your initial strategy. If you are looking for maximum market share and you see your costs going down in the future, you may establish pricing based on projected costs, not current costs. You had better be sure your projections are right.

When calculating your costs, add in the additional costs of doing business internationally. You should consider items like freight, duties, translation costs, and local staff costs. Some companies may choose to look at their international business as incremental to their base business in the United States. There is a good argument to support this view. You have already sunk cost into product development. If there are little or no additional product development costs incurred as a result of global expansion, consider the volume incremental. The caution is to make sure you have captured all the incremental costs associated with the volume.

You may have some internal organizational issues to address. There may be territorial issues with your sales force or distribution channels. If your pricing creates significant differences between countries, you will face gray-market activity. A gray market exists when the price of a product is lower in one country than another and a dealer or buyer finds a way to import the product into the target country and sell at a lower price than the authorized channels in that country. I discuss the gray market in more detail a bit later.

Another internal issue that may impact your strategy is transfer pricing. A transfer price is an internal price at which the U.S. company invoices the foreign subsidiary for the product shipped to that subsidiary for resale. It is a mechanism by which you place profit in one country or another to optimize your tax liability.

Because transfer pricing is almost exclusively a tax issue, it should have little impact on your resale pricing strategy. That is rarely the case, however, because human nature drives local managers to maximize their profit potential. If their costs, which are the transfer price from headquarters, are high, they will want to raise their resale prices to improve their local profits. In large companies, arguments about transfer pricing keep many people busy on a full-time basis.

The only real operational effect of transfer pricing relates to duties. Since duties are usually assessed on the landed cost of a product, the lower the landed cost, the lower the duties. If end users of your product are the importers, they will pay duty on their costs. If your distributor is the importer, he or she will pay duty based on a cost that is presumably lower than the end user's cost. Finally, if your subsidiary is the importer, duty is levied on a transfer cost that is lower than the distributor's cost. That has a real impact on total cost which, in turn, will affect pricing.

External Issues

The good news about internal issues is that you can control them. That is not the case with external forces that affect pricing. The most obvious external influence is competition. If your local competition has set a level of expectation in the mind of the local buyer, your pricing strategy must respond. This doesn't mean that you need to match every competitive price. It simply means that you need to know the current competitive pricing situation.

Your research will tell you what competition is doing as you enter a market. Your local team will keep you updated after your initial entry. The real trick is to make sure you understand what competitive pricing really is. That means you must understand not only the retail or resale price of the products but also the dealer or distributor pricing as well. You must know the features and functions of the competitive product so that your price makes sense to buyers when they compare your products to competitive products.

All three levels of pricing affect your strategy:

- *Suggested retail price (SRP) or, in a nonretail or consumer-oriented market, suggested resale price:* the "list" price

- *Street price:*   the price at which the product actually sells

- *Dealer price:*   the price the dealer pays to the manufacturer

What goes on below the surface of a competitor's pricing strategy is most important and not easy to discover. In Japan, NEC rarely, if ever, changes the suggested retail price (SRP) of its PC products. After introduction, the SRP stays the same throughout the life of a particular model. What changes is the dealer margin, which may start at 40% of SRP and, over time, move up to 60%. A dealer margin increase drives a lower street price for the product and keeps the volume of older products up as new products are introduced.

Local market conditions may dictate certain elements of your pricing policy. For example, if the local market is underpenetrated—there is a large available market with a low base of utilization of a product—you may choose to price your product low to create demand. If your product appeals to a niche in the market that values quality and brand appeal—snobbery—you may choose to price it high. Your research will show how many curious market conditions impact pricing.

There are governmental factors that will affect your pricing policy. The most onerous governmental influence is the duty rate. Governments use duties to raise money or exclude products from a market. Normally, the duty rates are reasonable because they pay for the customs and immigration costs of a government. The duty rate for computers imported into the European Community is 6%. The duty rate for importing personal items like jewelry or clothing into the United States is 10%. Comprehend this cost in your pricing strategy. It may create a disadvantage against those competitors who do not have to pay duty.

Duties can be exclusionary or punitive. In 1989, the U.S. government took action to discourage the import of color LCD (liquid crystal display) screens into the United States. Notebook PCs, among many other products, use these screens. At the urging of some companies here, U.S. Customs levied a duty of 70% to 160% on the panels from Japan. The argument was that the Japanese dominated in that slice of the market and U.S. companies wanted to be able to compete. To do so would take time and a lot of capital investment. If there were no imported products, these companies would have time to get their act together. In other words, keep the Japanese products out of the United States until local companies could compete.

The problem was that the scheme didn't work. IBM, Compaq, and Apple all told Customs that they would move manufacturing offshore if the government imposed these duties. The additional cost imposed by the excessive duty would require prices that were too high to stimulate demand for color notebook products. The duties were imposed, and the manufacturing of products using the panels, as well as the jobs involved, was moved offshore. It wasn't until 1993 that Customs actually reduced the duties to a reasonable rate. Then manufacturing moved back to the United States.

Other countries have imposed very high duties on some products. Argentina, for example, at one time had a 160% duty on PCs. Almost none were imported legally, and many were smuggled across the border. The rates soon came down, and products flowed freely and legally.

High duty rates lead to high prices for imported products. Many people try to beat the system by smuggling products across borders. And even more common is the practice of underinvoicing. As an example, assume the duty rate is 40% and the value of a product $1000. An importer who has an invoice showing that the product cost $500 can save $200 in cost (40% of $500). This practice is, of course, illegal. Customs officials are becoming more aware of the real value of foreign products. Importers who underinvoice can wreak havoc in a market where your local distribution and support channels follow the law.

GRAY MARKET

As you establish your pricing strategy, including your discounts to the distribution channels, you need to consider the effect of gray-market forces.

As I explained earlier, the unauthorized movement of goods across borders can cause many problems. If your product requires local support, you need to pay the entity that provides that support. One element of compensation to the supporters for warranty work is in the original margin they get from the sale of the product. If the product was purchased somewhere else and brought in by the buyer, the distributor doesn't get that margin. This adversely impacts his willingness to support the product.

If there is the slightest possibility of making money on a hot product, dealers will jump at it. An uplift in price in a foreign market not supported by real additional costs gives rise to this opportunity. Or, if the dealer margins in one market are significantly different from those in another, the incentive to participate in the gray market is present.

The early days of the PC industry provide a great example of how the gray market works. When demand was higher than supply, IBM published artificially high prices on PCs in Europe. The real cost of importing from the United States was around 8%–10%. The price uplift was between 15% and 18%. That meant that a PC dealer in England could buy from a dealer in the United States and make 5% to 10% profit with no risk and no investment.

THE PRICING STRATEGY

With this understanding of the factors that affect pricing, let's look at a few concepts involved in a pricing strategy.

The pricing strategy must comprehend several factors. Some issues depend heavily on the level of pricing under consideration. Suggested retail price can go a long way toward positioning your product. A high SRP may say that it is a high-quality product appealing to a limited set of buyers—a Mercedes. A lower price may generate a broader appeal—a Ford. Buyers will use price as one factor to determine what they think of a product.

Price may be a mechanism to increase profit or market share. If you want to maximize profit, raise the price. Unless you are selling in paradise, this may lead to lower volume. Even a company that sells gasoline in a country married to the automobile will drive the consumer to an alternative if the price is too high. But, if profit is the goal, have at it.

If you want to increase market share, lower the price.

Most markets have some price elasticity. There is a price point that will motivate buyers to buy more than they would at a higher point.

Going back to the example of Compaq in Japan, we can see how this may work. From 1983 to 1993, the growth in the Japanese PC market was very low compared to other markets in the world. It was in the range of 5% to 8% compounded annual growth rate (CAGR). At the same time, the world market was growing at 15% to 20% CAGR. The only exception to the pattern in Japan was 1989 to 1990, when notebook PC consumption accounted for 20% growth in the overall market. During that same period, however, desktop PC consumption tracked traditional patterns.

Pricing was a major reason for this low market growth. As I said earlier, a PC in Japan would cost about 30% more than in other markets. The prices of software were even higher. For example, in 1992, a spreadsheet application in Japan cost ¥98,000 (about $1000), although the same product, but with English-language support, sold in the United States for less than $300.

In October of 1992, Compaq introduced a range of low-priced PCs with SRPs in line with other world markets. This was only after Compaq had established an image as a quality provider of great products priced in line with the Japanese pricing model. The new products showed buyers that they could buy a good product at world-class prices.

Within three months of this action, all major PC providers in Japan—IBM, NEC, Toshiba, and Fujitsu—took pricing action. The pricing level of the entire market took a quantum leap downward. The market growth in 1993 was almost double that of the previous year. Certainly, there were other factors creating this new demand. The introduction of Microsoft Windows 3.1J was a major factor. But pricing was the real driver in the growth.

As you establish the correct relationship among the various levels of pricing—cost, dealer price, street price, and SRP—you also establish a mechanism to compensate the various entities in the food chain. The SRP will, in most cases, set the maximum price a distributor can charge a customer. If there are several tiers in the distribution channels, the available margin must compensate each tier for the value added to the sales and support process. If there is not enough margin, you must either remove tiers or reduce your profit. The obvious first choice for elimination is the link in the chain that adds the least amount of value. See Figure 9.1.

Sales Price

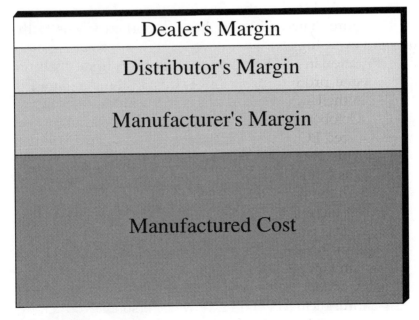

| Dealer's Margin |
| Distributor's Margin |
| Manufacturer's Margin |
| Manufactured Cost |

Figure 9.1 Margin structure.

The relative importance of discount structures varies from country to country. Many U.S. companies don't even use SRPs. They let the distribution channels and normal competitive factors dictate the end-user price. This is risky in that it takes away some control of the positioning of the product. But an effective communications plan will help restore your control of product positioning.

In other markets, many buyers want only a large discount off SRP. On my first sales call in Japan in 1976, I got a form from the purchasing agent of the company I was visiting. It had three questions on it. The first was: "What is your list price?" After the question was a blank space for a number. The second question was: "What is your normal discount?" Again, there was a blank for a number. Finally: "What is our discount?"

This company was not interested in the price it paid. It was interested in the discount it got. This was a way this company could know how important it was to the vendor.

Pricing can also be used to achieve corporate goals not related directly to profit but rather to the avoidance of cost. A prime example of this is in the automobile industry. At the end of each model year, car manufacturers reduce prices to clear out potentially obsolete inventory before they introduce the new model.

TECHNOLOGY

We tend to overlook the use of technology in the development of a pricing strategy. Many of us are so accustomed to using PCs with spreadsheets and databases that we tend to forget their power. Personal productivity tools can be very helpful in gathering, analyzing, and presenting pricing information. The combination of competitive pricing information with manufacturing costs and expenses in a spreadsheet can be a very power-ful "what if" tool.

Recently, on an airplane going from Tokyo to Dallas, I struck up a conversation with a fellow passenger. I noticed he had a notebook computer, and we talked about how we both use one. He was returning from a week-long negotiating session with a Japanese engineering firm that builds offshore oil rigs. They were trying to agree on a price for a major project in the Persian Gulf.

The pricing of this deal was very complex. A change in one factor affected several others. The negotiations dragged on for days. The process went something like this: The American team would make a proposal to the Japanese team. The Japanese team would go away for a day and come back with an answer, usually a counter-proposal. The American team would enter a few numbers into its PC and respond, usually with its own counterproposal. The eyes of the Japanese team members would roll back in their heads, and the team would retire for another day.

After several iterations of this process, my fellow traveler noticed that the Japanese team looked very tired. Over some *sake* that night, he learned that, each time the American team changed the deal, the Japanese team had to manually calculate a huge stack of ledgers using only a pencil and calculator. Only after hours of work could they analyze the impact of the proposed change. The American team used a PC and a spreadsheet to do the same thing in seconds.

The use of technology can give you a competitive edge. All my American friend had to do was to drag these negotiations on for a few more days, and the exhausted Japanese team would agree to anything.

Imagine what would have happened if the negotiators had needed a graphic presentation of the data! Most spreadsheets have some graphic capabilities, and most graphics packages have the ability to import spreadsheet data. The alternative manual process would surely have created an international incident.

This use of technology can be extremely helpful in analyzing and presenting large volumes of very complex pricing information.

Pricing, then, is one of the key elements in your overall plan for global expansion. Pricing for international markets requires consideration of issues that are not so important when you are selling only in the United States.

In the next chapter, we discuss some of the financial implications of the plan and how you can devise and execute a plan that will meet your financial goals.

10

So, How Do We Make Money at This?

In 1988, the government of Venezuela provided an incentive to local companies to import high-tech products like PCs. The incentive was a preferential exchange rate between the Venezuelan bolivar and the U.S. dollar. Stay with me on this—it gets a bit complicated, but it makes a good point. Here is how it worked.

The official exchange rate, published by the Central Bank of Venezuela, for the U.S. dollar was about 36 bolivars. In other words, if a Venezuelan company bought one U.S. dollar, it paid the bank 36 Bs. The exchange rate used for the import of PCs was about 18 Bs to the dollar. They could buy one U.S. dollar for 18 Bs. That meant, for example, that a company could buy a $2500 PC for 45,000 Bs but would have to pay 90,000 Bs for $2500 worth of another product, say, steel. This was a really good deal, and it did, in fact, increase the import of high-tech products.

Two other factors weighed heavily on the goodness of this deal. First, the Venezuelan economy was critically dependent on the price of oil. Oil was the major source of revenue and foreign currency. If oil sold for $20 per barrel, Venezuelans were smiling. At $8 per barrel, they weren't quite so happy.

The second factor had to do with cash. The Central Bank required that payment of goods with foreign currency, say U.S. dollars, be made with a 180-day letter of credit (LC). The local buyer would negotiate a deal with the U.S. supplier for the dollar price of goods. Let's keep the price at $2500. The Venezuelan Central Bank would then approve and guarantee a letter of credit to the U.S. supplier for $2500.

The supplier could take that LC to a U.S. bank and sell it at a discounted value and get his money immediately—no 180-day wait. The U.S. bank had no risk since the LC was in U.S. dollars and guaranteed by the Central Bank of Venezuela.

The Venezuelan company and the Central Bank then agreed that the company would pay the bank the 45,000 Bs ($2500 × 18 Bs per dollar) in 180 days. (All parties accounted for interest on money in all phases of this transaction, but I have eliminated this in this example. It is confusing enough.) At the end of 180 days, the Venezuelan company paid the Central Bank 45,000 Bs, and the Central Bank paid the LC holder $2500.

Because this incentive drove the local cost of high-tech products down, it also drove down prices. The theory was that lower prices would spur market demand. They did. Personal computer dealers in Venezuela were very aggressive in their pricing. In fact, they gave away almost all the savings they would have gained as a result of the currency incentive the government gave them. But the volume increased significantly, and everyone made a lot of money. This is the way it should have worked (see Figure 10.1). No problem, right? Wrong!

In the middle of all this, the price of oil dropped well below $10 per barrel. The government budget for 1988 was based on $13 per barrel. The Central Bank told all those PC dealers that they had only been kidding. The preferential exchange rates disappeared, and now the dealer had to pay the Central Bank 90,000 Bs for that $2500 LC. That, of course, was after the dealer had already sold the PC based on a cost of 45,000 Bs. Here is what actually happened (see Figure 10.2).

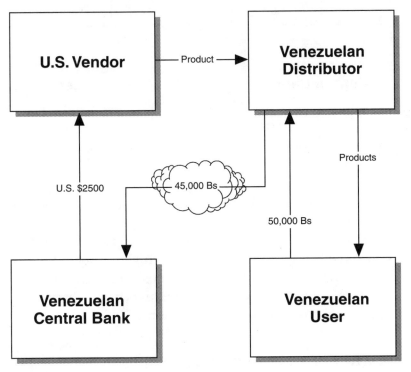

Figure 10.1 Exchange rate of 18 Bs to the U.S. $: net profit of 5000 Bs.

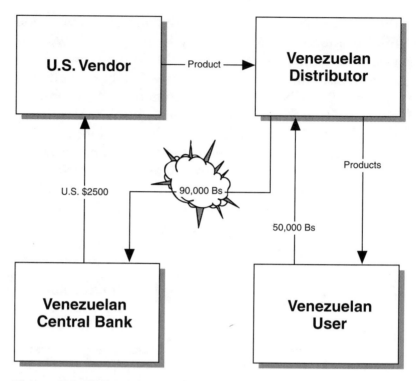

Figure 10.2 Exchange rate of 36 Bs to the U.S. $: net loss of 40,000 Bs.

Several dealers went bankrupt and several others almost did.

International business exposes you to new issues that you haven't faced in the past. In this chapter, we look at the impact global financial issues will have on your business, issues like currency fluctuation, countertrade, additional costs, and tax implications.

A Profit and Loss Model

Doing business in other countries is going to affect your business model. It is hoped revenue and profit will increase. But the lines on the P & L between the top and the bottom will change as well. The key to financial success is your ability to predict and manage those changes. Let's look at a typical P & L as shown in Table 10.1 to understand some of these differences.

Table 10.1 Typical P & L Statement

	Domestic	%	Int'l.	%
Revenue	$1,000.00	100	$1,150.00	100
Cost of goods sold (Material, labor, overhead, freight, duty)	500.00	50	525.00	46
Gross margin	500.00	50	625.00	54
Sales expenses	250.00	25	322.00	28
Marketing communications	30.00	3	46.00	4
General & administrative	50.00	5	80.50	7
Total expenses	330.00	33	448.50	39
Profit before tax	$ 170.00	17	$ 176.50	15

Let me explain some of the assumptions used in the pro forma statement of Table 10.1. The column headed "Domestic" is a look at a typical U.S. P & L statement. The column headed "Int'l." provides a view of the international piece of a global company's P & L. The columns headed "%" express the dollar amount as a percentage of revenue.

Let's look at the differences.

- *Revenue:* The pricing differences between different markets for the same product, as we discussed, will result in increased revenue. A 15% uplift is not unreasonable. This will vary, however, from country to country.

- *Cost of goods sold:* There will certainly be additional costs in freight and duty. There may be additional product costs. I have assumed a 5% addition to total cost.

- *Gross margin:*   The resultant international gross margin will be a bit higher than the domestic model.

- *Expenses:*   These will be higher for international business. We have already discussed the marketing and sales expenses. Later in this chapter, we discuss the general and administrative (G & A) expenses.

- *Profit before tax:*   The relative profit for international business can be a higher dollar amount but a lower percentage amount. Some companies call this *contributed margin* because all the headquarters and R & D expenses are not included in the international P & L. I discuss this a bit later in this chapter.

You may quibble about the specific numbers, and they will certainly change from company to company. But this model will serve us well for this discussion. Now, let's look at each line in a little more detail. This provides a good look at how you can manage your P & L for international business so that you actually achieve your financial goals.

REVENUE

Management of the revenue line is, of course, key to success. As the Venezuelan example at the beginning of this chapter shows, revenue isn't always as certain as it would appear. In all businesses, there are many factors that can change the volume results. In international business, there are some peculiar pitfalls that require close consideration.

Currency

Currency values fluctuate relative to each other on a constant basis. Say, the Japanese yen (¥) is trading at 104 to the U.S. dollar and that, two years ago, the rate was around ¥125 per dollar. If you are a U.S. company doing business in dollars, your revenue for the same volume over that period of time was increased by about 20% without your doing anything.

Don't get too excited—currency values can turn the other way very quickly. In the early 1980s, the dollar was very strong against European currencies. It got to almost one for one against the British pound and almost 3.6 to one against the German mark. At this writing, it is relatively weak—$1.65/£ and DM1.50/$. That situation would be okay if it were predictable, but it's not.

If you have a constant price in local currency—this is often a requirement driven by local competition—your revenue will move up and down based on the exchange rate. If you express your pricing in U.S. dollars, you or your distributor may become noncompetitive. You should decide which approach to take and then take steps to protect yourself.

If you are in the PC business or the automobile business, you should stick to selling PCs or cars. Let experts buy and sell currency. You can hedge your currency risk through a contract with your bank. Hedging simply means that you agree to provide a bank with a certain amount of a foreign currency at a given time in the future. The bank agrees to buy that amount of that currency from you at a guaranteed rate. By hedging, you can predict what your dollar income will be and be able to manage to that prediction.

Hedging, like any other banking service, is not free. Since the gain or loss in currency trading is real and the risk is great, the bank or currency trader wants sizable compensation. Think of it as legalized gambling. In each transaction, there is a winner and a loser. If 10 sellers are selling Mexican pesos at 2400 to the U.S. dollar, there are 10 buyers buying at that rate. The sellers and the buyers are constantly balancing their books and laying off their bets to cover the risk. Prices of the various currencies move accordingly.

What does all this mean to you? You need to cover your cost in currency transactions. Plan for it in your P & L, and share it with your distribution channels. If you work on the direct shipment model described in Chapter 7 or if you have a distributor who buys from you and sells for you in the local market, include a provision for currency fluctuations in your contract. It may be as simple as sharing the risk. In other words, if the value of the U.S. dollar goes up or down by more that 10% in a quarter, you will raise or lower the price by 50% of the fluctuation. There are many other schemes that will work as well.

If you are working through wholly owned subsidiaries, account for the translation gains and losses in your financial plan. The Financial Accounting Standards Board (FASB) has very specific rules on how you must keep track of all this. Check with your accounting people to get a full understanding of the requirements.

Of course, you can get into the buying and selling of foreign currencies on the open market as they become available to you. But realize that this is a different business than selling PCs or cars. You will need to adjust your expectations accordingly.

Countertrade

Many of the less-developed countries have difficulty trading with the economic powers of the world. The problem is that their local economy or their government policies prevent the open trading of their currencies. This may be caused by inflation or lack of internal resources or lack of reserves in a "hard" currency like the U.S. dollar or the British pound. Very few, if any, currency traders will deal in these "soft" currencies because of their volatility.

What do you do if you have an opportunity to sell your products in a country that has a highly volatile currency? One answer is to countertrade. Countertrade, or barter, was the basis of all business for centuries. A person who had something to sell found a buyer. The buyer had something to trade. They agreed on the amount, and the transaction was complete. The "currency" could have been cattle or pigs or shoes.

The countertrade system today is much more sophisticated, but the principle is the same. We don't hear a lot about it, but bartering is a fundamental element in some businesses in the United States today. It is not unusual, for example, to "buy" TV advertising time with products. Brokers are usually involved; they put together deals that may involve many different parties.

In the mid-1970s, Datapoint Corporation sold minicomputers to the Polish government. The government paid for the computers with pigs. The pigs were traded for shoes and the shoes for dollars. The first order of Compaq DespPro 386s we sold in the People's Republic of China was paid for in condoms. Of course, Compaq never saw the condoms—they were converted into dollars even before the sale was complete.

Countertrade is often helpful in getting around some of the bureaucratic nightmares that frequently surround transactions with less-developed countries. It may be easier to work out a countertrade deal than to get the appropriate approvals from all the necessary departments of the government.

Here are some keys to countertrade that you should consider:

- Get expert advice. Don't try this at home!

- Make sure the entire transaction is complete and documented before you proceed. That means that you get some guaranteed payment in dollars, or other hard currency, like a confirmed letter of credit, before you ship your product.

- Be prepared to pay a lot to the brokers. They make the deals and they broker the risks. Your pricing needs to reflect the broker's commission.

- Watch out for illegal dealings. Work with a reputable broker.

Countertrade is an effective and important method of doing business. If handled properly, it can be a great source of business in markets that otherwise would not be available to you.

COST OF GOODS SOLD

In Chapter 6, we discussed issues relating to product costs. There are just a few comments I would like to make here.

Remember to identify the additional product costs for doing business internationally. There may be document translation costs, packaging additions or additional things that you need to include in the shipment. But there are some less obvious costs to consider. For example, you will pay additional freight because of the distances covered. You pay duties to import products to foreign jurisdictions. There are administrative costs involved in the management of freight and duty issues.

One cost that needs serious consideration is warranty cost. Your warranty costs may be significantly higher in some foreign markets. First of all, make sure you understand the legal requirements for warranty. In the early 1980s, the standard warranty on a PC was 90 days. Most European countries, however, required a minimum of one year.

At Compaq, we had a heated discussion with the product development team regarding a specific product design. To minimize factory costs, the team wanted to attach the monitor rigidly to the rest of the unit. If the monitor broke, the service person would ship the entire unit—monitor and all—back to the factory. For safety and reliability reasons, monitors are usually not repaired in the field. You could take out the system board and the disk, but the rest had to be shipped back.

Calculations to determine the warranty costs did not include international costs. For trade within the United States, this strategy made some sense. But when you considered the costs of shipping a large unit across country borders, usually by air, the warranty costs became significantly higher.

First, there was the additional volume of space for the unit versus the monitor alone. When air freight is calculated, volume is important. Second, there is the hassle at the border. The duty would be higher since more "stuff" was being shipped. In some cases, in the People's Republic of China, for instance, it was cheaper to just scrap the monitor and ship a new one.

For many products, where repair and refurbishment of parts are commonplace, the duties paid on those spare parts are a significant cost. You pay duty on parts just as you do on complete units. Sometimes, after you have gone through a lot of paperwork and administrative tracking, you may retrieve the duties you paid on the part that was reexported back to the factory for repair. In many cases, however, the customs people will require the same serial number on the item to pay back the duty.

In some Asian and Latin American countries, you may never see the credit.

You should determine what these additional costs may be for your product and include them in the calculation of your warranty costs.

The pricing strategy should reflect these additional above-the-line costs, and your gross margin for international business should be higher than for domestic business. Be careful to judge how much higher. If the margins are too high, you may not be price-competitive, and you may encourage gray-market activity.

EXPENSES

In other chapters, we talk a bit about marketing, communications, distribution, and people expenses. There are a few miscellaneous expenses that will have an impact on the P & L, some of them minor, some not so minor. For example, look at office rent. This is usually a fairly routine expense, not a big issue. However, if you rent office space in many large cities around the world, like Mexico City or Tokyo, for instance, it will become an issue.

When the concept of NAFTA first became public— around mid-1990—the United States, Canada, and Mexico talked about 360 million consumers coming together in a $6.6 trillion free market. Landlords in Mexico City wanted to get their fair share of that little morsel of change. Rental rates for office space skyrocketed. The rates were so high that I got an impassioned plea from the general manager of Compaq's business in Latin America. He wanted me to hurry up and get started in Japan so that he would not have the most expensive office space in the company.

We did, in fact, rent the required amount of office

space in Japan. It was in a good location in Yotsua but not in an extravagant area like Ginza. For the privilege of renting a square foot of office space for one month, we had to pay more than it cost to build and own a square foot of comparable space in the headquarters campus in Houston. That's expensive!

The cost of office space in Japan is a result of their bubble economy, which has given rise to a ridiculous escalation in land prices. Let's look at the index that averages land prices in the six largest cities in Japan and rates them relative to a base year, in this case 1955, the year in which the index was begun; 1955 equals 100. That index in 1990 was 21,002! Just to put it in perspective, in the United States, the Consumer Price Index for the same period went from 100 in 1955 to 542 in 1990.

Financial Expenses

Some financial costs are higher when you do business internationally. For example, accounts receivable tend to be larger relative to revenue. The sense of urgency in paying invoices is not the same all over the world. In the United States, we expect to be paid in 30, maybe 45, days. In Italy, you can expect to wait 90 to 120 days. In some countries, the government will not allow payment in less than 180 days. Of course, you can sell your receivables so that you get your cash sooner, but that costs money and you need to plan for it.

Many times, it is not prudent to deal with international customers on an open account basis. Guaranteed letters of credit, confirmed on a U.S. bank, are often used as payment instruments. Again, there are fees involved in this kind of financial instrument. Most often, the buyer pays the fees at his end. But there are transfer fees at the seller's end as well. These fees are usually not excessive, but they are not trivial either. Check with your banker.

Hyperinflation

Another issue that will, in some way, affect your international business is hyperinflation. In the United States, Europe, and Japan, we have become accustomed to reasonable inflation rates, something on the order of 3% to 5% per year. In some countries, that number is more like 25%—per month! That is hyperinflation.

Most economists will agree that hyperinflation is caused by the government printing too much money too fast. But, rather than dwelling on the causes of hyperinflation, over which you have no control, let's look at the results and what you can do about them.

The first thing affected by hyperinflation is pricing. We can measure the effects of inflation in our everyday lives by comparing the cost of anything today versus that of 20 years ago. Imagine having that kind of increase in one month! In countries that suffer from this problem, pricing is almost always indexed against U.S. dollars. In fact, in some countries, such as Argentina, you can actually take out a mortgage on your house using dollars as the currency.

Hyperinflation also affects wages and salaries. Again, indexing against some hard currency like dollars is the preferred method of addressing the issue. The salaries of employees are often paid in local currency but are expressed in U.S. dollars. When the actual money is paid, the amount of local currency paid is based on the current exchange rate in dollars.

Pricing and salaries can easily be adjusted for inflation. Where hyperinflation really hurts is in the value of local assets. Imagine what happens to receivables and cash in such an environment. By the way, hyperinflation has little or no effect on capital assets. Their value is intrinsic. Liquid assets, on the other hand, are tied to the value of the currency in which they are stated. One way to minimize the effect is to minimize the investment. Fund your receivables through borrowings from local banks, and convert them to hard currency as soon as you can.

TAX IMPLICATIONS

One of the major issues in doing business around the world is tax. Every government wants your money. They dream up all sorts of ingenious schemes to get it. The rate at which they take it varies from country to country. Your job is to minimize the amount of tax you have to pay. Of course, most governments will say you have to pay their rates for income earned—or whatever measure they impose—in their country. There are some things you can do.

Intercompany transfer pricing is a good tool to help move income—and, therefore, tax liability—from one country to another. If you sell product in Europe, for example, that corporate income tax rate may be higher than in the United States. Therefore, the higher the price at which you sell product to your local subsidiary, the lower their profit. The lower their profit, the lower their tax. You get the picture.

As you might imagine, there are limits to what you can do. The tax authorities in those countries with high tax rates will be very interested in your transfer pricing policies. For example, you will almost certainly have to sell the same product to each subsidiary at almost the same price. Justifiable price differences need to be supported by defensible cost differences.

The government of the United States wants to help. In order to promote exports, the IRS has established a mechanism by which you can reduce your U.S. tax liability. It is called the Foreign Sales Corporation, or FISC. This is a subsidiary operation of your company that is organized under the laws of a foreign country or possession of the United States. Your U.S. company sells product to your FISC, and your FISC sells to your other subsidiaries or your distributors and dealers.

If you set this corporation up properly and use it properly in the transaction of sales to international customers, you can save a lot of tax dollars.

All tax issues are of the "don't-try-this-at-home" variety. Make sure you get expert advice to set up and manage your operations to minimize your tax liability.

TECHNOLOGY TO THE RESCUE

At this level of operations, in the guts of your company, technology provides tools that are now essential to running the business. All the core financial systems available to manage your business come into play here: forecasting systems, accounting and payroll systems, and banking systems. In addition, there are a few things you may not have considered.

One of the key advantages of a local subsidiary is local billing to customers in local currency. That doesn't mean, however, that you need accounting people in every subsidiary location. Many companies in Europe have central accounts receivable and accounts payable operations. With sophisticated networks and telephone systems, you don't need an administrative staff in the

City of London or on the Champs Élysées in Paris or in the Bahnhofstraße in Zurich. You can put a staff of multilingual people in Luxembourg or Holland where rent is low and communications are good.

You don't need local inventory in each subsidiary location. You can have a regional inventory that can be managed through an inventory management system. This central inventory system can feed the central billing system with the data necessary to generate the invoice.

The point is that, through creative use of readily available technology, you can easily manage your cost of doing business in many countries. Invest the time and effort to understand what is available, and seriously consider using it.

The entire subject of profit and financial management depends heavily on the goals and the culture of your company. In this chapter, I have highlighted some issues that you should consider in the planning and management of your international business.

In the next chapter, we look at the issues surrounding your most valuable resource—your people—and how management of that human resource is different in different countries.

11

The Heart and Soul of the Enterprise: The People

Apple Computer began selling its products in Japan through a distributor, Canon. Soon afterward, Apple opened a subsidiary. That was in 1983. From 1983 to 1989, Apple's market share in Japan grew from 0% to 0%—not a very dramatic performance! During that same period, Apple had five American presidents of Apple Japan.

In 1989, Apple hired Shigechika Takauchi as the president of Apple Japan. Takauchi-san had spent many years at Toshiba, a major PC vendor in Japan, before joining Apple. He was—and still is—Japanese. From 1989 to 1993, Apple's market share in Japan grew from 0% to 13.4%. According to International Data Corporation, in 1993, Apple was the second-largest provider of PCs in Japan, behind only NEC. A remarkable performance in only four years!

What's the difference? Certainly, there are many contributing factors—that kind of result doesn't come from a single cause. Apple paid a lot more attention to broadening its distribution channels after Takauchi-san arrived. It localized its entire product line in Japan. It grew its staff in Japan. But the real difference was the head of Apple Japan.

During the terms of the first five presidents of Apple Japan, communications with the home office were great. Communications with the market, however, were not so great. These were not bad people; these were not stupid people. They just weren't Japanese. With Takauchi-san, just being Japanese certainly wasn't enough. He was a capable executive, and he put Apple in a much better position to understand the real market requirements of this very complex market. With that understanding, and with a stronger commitment to respond to those requirements, Apple's performance improved dramatically.

People make companies run. Dealing with human resources in foreign countries is very different, however. This is not to say that the skills developed for managing people in the United States don't apply—they do. But there are significant cultural and legal differences that have to be comprehended in the plan.

In this chapter, we look at ways to find, attract, compensate, and motivate people to manage the international business, both at home and abroad. We investigate the organizational impact of dealing with many different languages and cultures. Finally, we discuss some ideas on how to set up the communications links—both telecommunications and interpersonal—that are so vital to a global business.

THE AMERICAN WAY

Before we talk about specific areas of human resource management, let me first describe some differences between American companies and companies in other cultures as they relate to people. The relationship between the employer and the employee is not the same all over the world.

In the United States, the company exists for the benefit of the shareholders, the people who own the stock in the company. It doesn't matter whether the company is privately held or publicly traded. The shareholders put up the equity, and they expect and deserve compensation. They empower a board of directors to manage the business for them. The board maintains a fiduciary relationship with the people who elect them, making decisions that are in the best interests of the shareholders.

The model is a bit different in other countries. In Japan, for example, the company exists for the stakeholders. The definition of stakeholders includes shareholders. It also includes banks, customers, vendors, and employees. These groups have a stake in the company and are interested in the well-being of the enterprise.

The board of directors of an American company might measure the CEO's performance based on revenue, profit, earnings per share, or asset utilization. Although these are important measurements for all companies, the Japanese CEO might be more interested in market share, customer satisfaction, or employee harmony.

Another way to show the difference in the relationship between employer and employee is to look at labor disputes. In the United States, a strike involves workers walking out on the job, forming a picket line, and refusing to go back to work until their demands are met. Such a strike may go on for days, months, or even years. Strikes by foreign workers may be a little different.

On my very first trip to Italy, the airline workers, the hotel workers, and the garbage workers were all on strike. In addition, the plant workers at the factory I was visiting were also on strike. The garbage workers marched outside my hotel in the early morning. By mid-morning, when I had arrived at the plant, the workers there were marching through the offices every hour on the hour, banging lids of garbage cans. It was difficult to work there, so we moved the meeting to my hotel. Even though the hotel workers were on strike, we held the meeting in relative peace. I could not leave Milan that night because the airlines were all shut down. But, the next day, everything was back to normal—all the strikes were over.

I happened to be in Paris during a general strike in 1976. The French approach their strikes a bit differently. They don't begin until 9 a.m., after everyone has had a chance to get their morning coffee and make it to work. The strike is halted at about noon, so that everyone can go to lunch, and is resumed at about 2 p.m. It is over by 5 p.m., so that everyone can go home. This general strike included a complete shutdown of the city—no electricity, no work, nothing.

In Japan, a strike may only involve workers wearing armbands with slogans printed on them. The Japanese continue to work while making their protest silently.

This approach to strikes results in some interesting numbers of days lost due to labor disputes. The Keizai Koho Center in Japan has compiled the number of man-days lost from labor disputes in various countries. Here are the numbers for 1989:

United States	16,996,000
Italy	4,436,000
United Kingdom	4,128,000

France	805,000
Japan	176,000
Germany	100,000

Now, let's look at a few issues related to hiring the right people for the job.

THE RIGHT PERSON FOR THE HEADQUARTERS JOB

You will need someone in your headquarters assigned to manage your new international business. You may choose an internal candidate for the job, or you may decide to recruit outside your company. In either event, there are some attributes about the candidate that you should require. Let me offer a few suggestions.

Make sure the candidate is flexible and willing to do things differently—an out-of-the-box thinker. The candidate must have really thick skin and a lot of determination. Both will be required. The candidate should have, or be able to get, the respect of fellow workers because he or she will ask them to do things they don't understand and won't want to do. International experience, of course, is always an asset for any candidate. An understanding of other cultures and business systems will make your job easier. Familiarity with languages other than English is helpful.

Of course, the person should be willing and able to work odd hours—your customers will not be in the same time zone as your main office—and must be willing and able to travel. After the initial attraction of going to foreign places wears off, travel becomes a burden that must be managed.

Finally, make sure your headquarters person is capable of making decisions and is empowered to execute the plan.

The Right Team for the Local Office

Key to success in any enterprise are the local teams of people who represent your company in the various countries around the world. Finding, hiring, and managing those people will present some challenges to you.

Identifying the Candidates

An American employer who wants to find a midlevel manager or an individual contributor usually runs an ad in the newspaper or turns to an employment agency to search for candidates. If, on the other hand, that company is looking for a CEO, the process is quite different. The board of directors may engage an executive search firm. It may have a closely targeted list of candidates it wants to approach. The approach may be very indirect —someone knows someone who knows the brother-in-law of the candidate. The approach is always discreet and private.

In other cultures around the world, recruiting for positions much lower in the organization is more like the "CEO" style. The relationship between the employer and the employee is quite different. We discuss this later in this chapter. As a result of these differences, midlevel managers will not respond to newspaper ads and will not put their résumés in the hands of an agency. They look for a job in a very guarded manner. In their search, they often respond very well to cautious approaches by friends and very good executive search firms.

The indirect, discreet approach to recruiting may be more expensive and will certainly take more time than the direct approach. Good judgment must be applied. Don't engage an expensive executive search firm to find an individual contributor that is not critical to your success. But be prepared to spend a lot of money and a lot of time to get that key player. Many international executive search firms charge a retainer of 30% to 40% of the anticipated first year's income for the job candidate. That retainer is usually paid up front and does not include expenses.

Let me offer a bit of advice that you should consider very seriously. Take the time and spend the money necessary to find the right person to be the leader of the local team. If you get the wrong person in the job, you will both regret it.

Another suggestion: Just because a candidate speaks good English doesn't mean that he or she can do the job. In fact, in some countries, you may not be able to find qualified people who speak English. Of course, at high levels in the organization, communications with the home office are essential, and English is usually the language used to communicate among subsidiaries of American companies. But many people on a local team don't need to talk to headquarters. Determine which jobs really require fluency in English. Then, for the other jobs, make English a desirable skill but not a requirement.

Recruiting

After you have identified the right candidates for the local jobs, you need to persuade them to join the team. In some cases and in some cultures, this may be very easy. A job candidate may be very excited about your company or your products. The opposite may also be true. Remember that you are an American company. That means a lot in many countries around the world. And that meaning may not always be favorable.

Regardless of which country you are considering, other American companies have been there before you. Some of those companies have not done a very good job. They move in, hire people, fail in their efforts, and fire everyone. Or they hire too many people at the beginning and have to fire a few people. Local workers, at all levels, know this. Because of the negative impressions left by the actions of your predecessors, some of those workers are not really interested in working for an American company.

If you are able to overcome the image hurdle, there are a few other things you should consider. Make sure that your job offers conform to local practice. In Japan, for example, it is normal for a company to provide the higher-level people a low-interest loan so that they can buy a house or apartment. When they leave a company, those loans come due. You need to understand this practice and be responsive to it.

In many countries, prospective employees are very sensitive to the opinions of their friends and family, more so than in the United States. It is possible that you may reach an agreement with a candidate, only to find that his friends talked him out of taking your job offer. This happened to me once when I was hiring people in Japan. The candidate had agreed to all the terms in the job offer. He went to talk to his friends, and they convinced him not to go to work for an American company.

The Japanese system of employment presents some particularly difficult competition for non-Japanese companies. Japanese industry believes in recruiting people right out of college. Most companies have a "freshman" class that is recruited in March or April and comes to work in June. The "class" meets in a room where the president of the company welcomes them with a motivational speech.

Members of this "class" stick together throughout their employment at the company, which usually lasts a long time. Lifetime employment, so famous in Japan in the past, is no longer absolute. People do change jobs, either on their own or at the company's insistence. The norm, however, is that an employee stays with a company throughout his or her career.

COMPENSATION

As you start to deal with international business, you will be faced with many compensation issues. For example, in the United States, we normally pay people a base salary and sometimes a bonus or an incentive, depending on the job. We make mandatory and discretionary contributions to benefit funds such as social security and retirement funds. We differentiate the compensation among our workers based on the job content, the performance of the incumbent, and the length of service of the incumbent. The mix of these elements changes from company to company and from job to job.

In other cultures, there are different elements in the compensation package. For example, in many European countries, the base salary may be lower than in the United States, but the benefits may be significantly higher. Most companies give all employees, regardless of how long they have been with the company, four or five weeks of vacation. Vacations are almost always taken during July and August.

In Singapore, government and industry meet once a year to determine the "suggested" salary increases to be given by employers. The raise is the same nationwide and given to all employees. Employees are also given a "thirteenth" month of salary. This, again, is applied across the board to all employees.

In Japan, many companies provide subsidized housing for employees because the entire relationship between employer and employee is much more like that of a family. Employers provide additional allowances based on the number of children an employee has. They also provide allowances for travel to and from work and a bonus—considered a gift—twice a year. These bonuses are based on a percentage of the employee's salary. The percentage, determined by the management based on company performance, is the same for everyone. These are not merit bonuses but gifts from the company. They are given at about the same time the summer gift, the *ochugen,* and the winter gift, the *oseibo,* are exchanged among friends and family members throughout Japan.

The members of each "class," as described in the previous section, are paid about the same salaries. Up to fairly high levels in the company, there is little differentiation among workers based on anything but seniority. On the basis of a worker's age alone, you can make a fairly accurate guess at the salary paid that person and the level of responsibility, regardless of what the job is or where the employee works.

Expatriate Programs

The chances are good that you will eventually want someone from your headquarters staff to move to a foreign country for an extended period of time. This is helpful in setting up a local organization or in creating effective communications links between the subsidiary and the home office. Most workers in this situation are paid on an expatriate plan.

The purpose of an expatriate plan is to compensate the employee for the extra cost and aggravation of living overseas. Some companies have allowed these plans to become a way for employees to make a lot of money in a short period of time. That approach usually leads to disappointment on the part of the employer—the cost is usually too high for the benefit received.

Because it usually costs an expatriate more than a local person to live in a country, the expatriate program typically includes a cost-of-living allowance, a housing allowance, and a school allowance. In addition, because there is often income taxation by more than one government, there is an allowance for additional taxation. Many companies pay for professional preparation of the employee's tax returns. Usually, the employee and his or her family come home once a year at company expense.

It doesn't take a CPA to figure out that expatriate programs can become very expensive. As an employee remains overseas for many years, the cost becomes prohibitive. The company ends up paying the employee for additional taxes. That payment is taxed and, ultimately, the company is paying taxes on taxes on taxes.

For a reasonable period of time, say, two years, an expatriate can provide invaluable service to the start-up of a subsidiary. You should consider the potential benefit to the company as well as the costs.

THE ORGANIZATION

Business organizations are going through tremendous change. Trends are emerging that affect the way we do business. For example, in the traditional organization, we align people according to function. We have a sales department, a manufacturing department, an engineering department, and so on. As businesses are pressured to change—to respond to competition, for example—they are forced to become more efficient. As a result, more and more organizations are moving toward the team approach, in which people from many different functions are assigned to a particular process.

Because so many companies are expanding their businesses outside the United States, we see a movement toward the borderless organization, the truly global company. Instead of having all R & D, engineering, and manufacturing, for example, in the home location, many companies are cloning those organizations in foreign markets. And they are organizing the company so that the international business can function as, and be measured as, a complete business unit.

Finally, many organizations have changed because technology has made those changes in the workgroup possible. I will discuss the technology in the next section. The organizational impact of technology is significant, however. Technology allows us to have knowledge workers anywhere in the world collaborating with one another on a project. They can share knowledge anytime, anywhere.

THE RULES OF THE GAME

In the United States, we have a fairly well-defined set of rules governing the relationship between employer and employee. We have rules about how people are paid, about discrimination based on a variety of factors, about the safety and well-being of the employee, and about the employer's right to hire and fire. Don't expect the same rules in other countries.

It is significantly more difficult to fire people in most

countries outside the United States. That is one reason why people are not hired as quickly as we expect. In many European companies, workers sit on an advisory board of the company and have significant input into how the company is managed. In many developing countries, where the concept of employees' rights is less developed, employees are treated much differently than in the United States or Europe.

The American sense of fair play in the area of discrimination doesn't necessarily apply all over the world. Racial and sex discrimination is commonplace in many countries. Trying to impose U.S. human resource policies in every country around the world will lead to frustration and disappointment.

The issue of rules of employment is another "don't-try-this-at-home" issue. Make sure you get good professional advice when entering this area. You will find that the extra time and effort are well spent in getting it right the first time.

TECHNOLOGY

One of the reasons why so many companies are expanding outside the United States is that technology provides us with so many tools that make working in a global environment possible. As I mentioned earlier in the book, knowledge is the currency of the future. Knowledge is, or will become, the largest asset of many companies. Technology provides us with ways to share and develop that internal knowledge to create a competitive advantage.

With all the changes in your organization that will occur because of your expansion, your people will require some basic tools like E-mail and voice mail. You may already have these tools available. Some of the more advanced tools will become important as you develop your organization.

Groupware is an emerging technology that may already play an important part in your company's business. *Groupware* is a term coined to describe a set of technologies used to make people working in groups more productive. Those people may be in the home office, or they may be spread all over the world. Groupware applications allow those team members to share knowledge and communicate easily to exchange information in building the knowledge base of the company.

Portable and even wireless computing has provided the road warrior with a way to keep connected to the base of knowledge in the company. International road warriors are presented with unique challenges in dealing with foreign phone companies, but some countries, like the United Kingdom and France, provide communications capabilities. Just make sure you carry a lot of modems with you. Because of the different phone systems around the world, one modem will not work worldwide.

You may find different levels of resistance to technology in different countries. In the United States, the manager and the business professional and the knowledge worker of today are all quite comfortable with technology. That may not be the case in many European countries. For example, it may not be chic for a senior manager in Germany to be seen typing on a keyboard. This is a job reserved for secretaries. In China, office automation is not yet an issue since technology is still more expensive than applying more people power to the task at hand.

As you develop your organization around the world, be sensitive to these differences, and try to move the workers toward a good understanding of what technology can do for them.

There are so many issues revolving around the heart and soul of your enterprise. Here, I have touched on a few that you should consider when planning and executing your global expansion. Spend the time and effort necessary to understand the rules and customs of each country you enter so that you can take full advantage of this most valuable resource—your people.

In the next chapter, we look at some of the little, and not so little, things that will allow you to succeed in the international world.

12

*Around the World
in 80 Minutes*

In his fourth inaugural address, delivered on January 20, 1945, Franklin Delano Roosevelt provided us with some food for thought about our position in the world today. He said:

> We have learned that we cannot live alone, at peace; that our own well-being is dependent on the well-being of other nations, far away. We have learned that we must live as men, and not as ostriches, nor as dogs in the manger. We have learned to be citizens of the world, members of the human community.

After all the effort you have spent in creating your plan, you are ready to step up and become a citizen of the world. Now, you need to spend a little time and effort to understand some of the little, and not so little, things that will make or break the payoff to all the resources already invested. In this chapter, we look at answers to such burning questions as:

- How do you give your business card to a Japanese businessman?

- In Europe, why doesn't anyone answer the phone in August?

- How come nobody showed up for the meeting I scheduled for 10 a.m. in Panama?

FIRST THINGS FIRST

Before you actually begin to execute your plan, there are a few basic tools you need. For example, you need to communicate with prospective customers or distributors. Using the phone to do that isn't quite what it is in the United States. In addition, you will need a passport to travel abroad. Here are a few hints about these basic tools.

The Telephone

In order to execute your plan, you need to communicate with people in the real international world, in the (please, excuse the expression) global village. That means telephones and that means travel.

Dealing with the telephone as a communications tool is a bit different with international business. First of all, you have to contend with different time zones. If you decide to call a prospective customer in Hong Kong during the middle of your workday, you will get either no answer, if you call his office, or an irate customer, if you call his home. When it is noon in Chicago—you can figure your time from there—it is 2 a.m. in Hong Kong. A list of the time zones of various cities around the world can be found in the Appendix.

There is another difference in calling internationally. First, you dial 011 instead of just 1 to get an international line. Then, you dial the country code, the city code, and the number. To get the right telephone number, just look on the customer's letterhead or business card. But be careful. The assumption behind most printed phone numbers is that the caller is dialing within the country. Look at your own letterhead. In most countries around the world, the city code is preceded by a zero. For example, if you look at a business card from London, the number may be 041-555-5555. If you are calling from the United States, omit the leading zero. So, if you are dialing that London number from the United States, dial 011-44-41-555-5555. I have included a list of country and city codes in the Appendix. In those countries not listed, check with the U.S. operator to see if that country has direct dial access.

When you finally do get through, remember that you will probably be talking to someone whose native language is not English. I discuss language later in this chapter.

Don't be surprised if the reception over the phone line is not as good as you expect at home. In some of the less-developed countries, the quality of the phone systems is not very good. You will get static, and you will often get disconnected.

The Passport

If you travel outside the United States, you'll need a passport. Some proof of citizenship, like a voter's registration card, will work for Canada and Mexico, but a passport is always better. Look in your local phone book in the "U.S. Government" pages. Under the Department of State, you should find a listing for the U.S. Passport Agency. Call them up and ask for an application for a passport. Here's what you'll need:

1. Proof of citizenship: either a certified copy of your birth certificate or your certificate of citizenship or naturalization

2. Two identical front-view photos, 2 inches × 2 inches. You can get these at many photo shops; look in the phone book for passport photos.

3. Proof of identity: a driver's license or a state-issued ID card

4. A completed Form DSP 11, which you can get at the passport agency or have mailed to you

5. $65 in exact cash, check, or money order

After you get all that together, you must appear in person at the passport agency to apply. Fortunately, getting a passport renewed is a little easier. A U.S. passport lasts for 10 years, so you won't have to renew very often.

GETTING READY FOR THE FIRST TRIP

As you prepare for what may be your first overseas business trip, spend a little time getting to know something about the country you are going to visit. Get out an atlas and find out where the country is, what the neighboring countries are, and what time zone it is in. In addition, find out some facts about the demographics, the politics, and the economy. These will be useful in introductory and nonbusiness conversations.

For example, what is the difference between Holland and the Netherlands? Holland is a part of the Netherlands, as California is a part of the United States. When you refer to the country, it is the Netherlands, not Holland. How are England, Great Britain, and the United Kingdom related? Great Britain includes England, Scotland, and Wales. If you add Northern Ireland, you have the United Kingdom. If you want to appear egregiously groovy, just say the UK. If you go to Argentina, don't call those islands the Falklands—they're the Malvinas. Make sure you don't confuse the Republic of China—Taiwan—with the People's Republic of China (PRC).

It is all right to be new at this sort of thing. It is okay to ask questions of your hosts, who will most probably be delighted to educate you about their country. Just keep an open mind, and try to learn as much as you can. Showing an interest in local culture, history, language, or politics is a good way to build a relationship with your foreign colleagues.

THE BUSINESS CARD

The business card is one of the most useful introductory tools you can have. It provides a lot of information about you and your company. It should have your name, your title, your address, your telephone and fax numbers and, if you are really connected, your Internet address. It should contain the name and logo of your company. It should be professionally prepared and printed. This may be the first piece of documentation your customer or host will have from you. Get it right.

In some countries where English is not commonly spoken, it is helpful to have the pertinent information printed on the back of your card in the local language. This is particularly helpful in countries like Japan, Taiwan, the People's Republic of China, or Thailand. Just make sure that the translation is professionally done. You don't want a silly or offensive translation on your business card.

You should also be sure a translation is appropriate for the country you are visiting. In the mid-1980s, I was working in Asia. I spent a lot of time in China, Hong Kong, and Singapore. I had my name and other relevant information printed on the back of my cards in Chinese. During a trip to Indonesia, I was paying a courtesy visit to the Minister of Finance. Compaq had just landed a big order for PCs from his agency, and I wanted to thank him for his business.

When I arrived at his office, I greeted him and handed him one of my cards. I proudly pointed out the reverse side of the card, where the Chinese translations were printed. He looked at me in a very curious way—not at all pleasant—and put the card away. We continued with the meeting.

After we left the meeting, I asked my colleague about the business card exchange. He told me that it is illegal to have anything with Chinese characters in Indonesia. The Indonesians are so concerned about the political influence of the PRC that they do not allow the language represented in any way in their country. If you go to a Chinese restaurant, the menu is in Indonesian and English, not Chinese.

Our treatment of business cards is a bit more casual than it is in other cultures. You should give and receive a card seriously and with dignity. When you get the other person's card, read it. Don't just stick it in your pocket. Like yours, that card represents some important information about the person you are visiting. Don't take notes on it and, whatever you do, don't pick your teeth with it!

What Was Your Name Again?

You will find foreign names confusing and hard to pronounce. Don't give up on it. Remember, that person's name is just as important to him or her as your name is to you. One reason to read a business card is to see the name printed. That often helps to understand and recall the pronunciation. If you still don't get it, ask again. It is better to ask a few times than to mispronounce the name.

Most cultures are more formal in their interrelationships than ours. In the United States, we almost immediately jump to the less formal form of address and call people by their first names. Don't presume that it is acceptable to do so. Stick to the surname until you have been invited to do otherwise.

Many experienced international business professionals understand your quandary about names. They are used to dealing with Americans and almost immediately ask you to use their first name. A very good friend of mine in Indonesia is named Eddy Sariaatmadja. As we were introduced and shook hands, he told me to call him Eddy. Thank goodness!

When we write our names in the United States, we write our given names, followed by our surname. That is not the case all over the world. In most Asian countries, the surname is first, followed by the given names. The VP and General Manager of the Asia/Pacific Division of Compaq is named Lim Soon Hock. It took me a long time to convince people at the home office that he was not Mr. Hock, but Mr. Lim.

In Latin countries, both Latin American and European, the father's surname is followed by the mother's surname. For example, the late Spanish leader's full name is Francisco Franco Bahamonde. We know him as Franco. The leader of Colombia is Cesar Gaviria Trujillo, President Gaviria.

LANGUAGE

The use and abuse of language provide us with a constant supply of annoyance and amusement. It is one of the basic things that separates us from other countries, and yet it is the most important tool through which we communicate. As Americans, we are not often confronted with the problem of language. Most of the people we deal with speak English.

Some countries, because of size and geography, must cope with more than one language. The closest to us is Canada, which has both French and English as official languages. Belgium recognizes Flemish and French as official languages, while Switzerland uses French, German, Italian, and Romansch. In the People's Republic of China, where there are hundreds of dialects of Chinese, oral communication between citizens of different provinces is often impossible—they don't recognize one another's language. However, because Chinese characters are ideograms, the written language is common.

As you begin to communicate with people whose native language is not English, there are a few things to keep in mind. First of all, speak slowly and enunciate your words. You don't have to speak louder. Foreign people are not, by nature, hard of hearing. But speaking slowly helps them to really "hear" what you are saying.

Try to learn a few words of the language of the country you are visiting. Learn to say "hello" and "thank you" or something simple like that. I know how to order a beer and ask where the bathroom is in seven languages. By the way, don't ask for the bathroom—that's where you take a bath. Ask for the toilet or the WC (water closet). People in other countries are often pleased to know that you are interested in their language and are willing to try to learn a few words and phrases.

Of course, if you have the time and the aptitude, learn to speak a foreign language fluently. That will be a tremendous help in your business dealings. Be aware of your level of fluency, however, because you can get yourself into trouble. A friend of mine speaks seven languages fluently but will do business in only two of them.

If you don't speak a language at the same or similar level of fluency as the person with whom you are dealing, either get a translator or speak English. Most foreign business professionals understand English very well although they may not be as comfortable speaking it. If language presents a barrier, get a translator. If your associate speaks good English, use English. It is much better for you to speak good English than bad Japanese.

It works the other way as well. I was taking a friend from Japan to dinner in a restaurant with an Australian theme. He said he wanted to wash his hands before dinner and asked where the toilette was. I pointed in the general direction and he left. After about 10 minutes, I started to get worried. The place was not very crowded at the time, so there was no particular reason why it should take so long. Just then, he returned. I asked what took so long. He explained that the door to one room had the word "Blokes" on it and the other door had the word "Shielas," a clever Australian way of saying men and women. He didn't know what the words meant and waited until he saw someone go into the "Blokes" before he could determine which room was which.

The mixing of languages can be amusing. During a visit to Zurich, I went with some friends to have dinner at a place that was a combination bar and cafe. There was live music from a small band. It was a lively, light-hearted environment.

All men in Switzerland must spend some time in the military. The boot camp is a six-month ordeal up in the mountains. When the six months are up, the soldiers are given a short leave. One of these soldiers was in the restaurant that night. He was clearly celebrating his "release."

As the night wore on, and he could hardly walk, he went to the table next to us and, speaking in German, asked one of the American women to dance with him. She replied, in English, that she did not speak German. He responded, in perfect English, "I am sorry, I don't speak French." He then fell over backward and was dragged out of the bar.

While at Compaq, I hosted many different international visitors. An interesting event occurred during a visit by our German dealers. Most people at Compaq who met customers, say, at a trade show or during one of these dealer visits, had brass badges with their names on them. The security people had similar badges. But, instead of their names, the badges read "Loss Prevention" to show these people were part of the security team.

One feature of this dealer visit was a plant tour. A guide led the group of 15 people, and one of the Compaq German salespeople walked along with me. As we left the plant, the salesman turned to one of the security people and said, "Thank you, Loss."

You have heard that the English and the Americans are separated only by a common language. A British friend was visiting my office. We had arranged for me to take him to the airport at the end of the day. It turned out that another person was going to the airport and, to save me a trip, he offered to drive my friend. My friend went to my secretary and asked for the keys to my car. He said to her, "My kit is in his boot." She looked at him as if he was from Mars and looked at me to translate. I told her his luggage was in my trunk and he needed to get it out.

During one of my visits to England, I had a chance to play golf at Wentworth, near London. My wife had just bought me a golfing outfit, a pair of knickers. As I emerged from the locker room, I asked my friends what they thought of my knickers. They broke out laughing. The trousers I had on are called *plus fours* in England. Knickers are women's underwear.

We constantly use idioms in our everyday speech. I have written down just a few of the hundreds of idioms I have heard today.

- Don't end up with egg on your face
- Fit to be tied
- Can't get to first base
- Hit the nail on the head
- Let's get this straight
- The party is over
- Chasing rainbows
- Getting into gear
- Thumbs up on that

I think you get the point. Imagine how someone who doesn't speak English as a native language would interpret these words. As you speak to people, try to avoid the use of idioms or colloquialisms. It will only muddy the waters and drive the listener bananas.

Finally, you should know that humor doesn't always translate well. Telling jokes that turn on a word or phrase are very difficult for foreigners to understand. Of course, there are situations that are just plain funny, and you will encounter many people with a great sense of humor who will appreciate those situations. But, on the other hand, don't be disappointed if the jokes you tell don't get the expected response.

WHAT'S FOR DINNER?

Traveling to foreign places presents us with many opportunities to taste different foods. If you are not an adventurous eater, be prepared to suffer. If you are willing to try new things, be prepared to be pleasantly, and sometimes not so pleasantly, surprised. In many cultures, a meal is a very important part of the day. It is a time when people get together to share food and their experiences of the day. This is not so different from the United States, but the level of intensity is a bit higher. Many foreign cultures don't subscribe to the Emily Post style of eating. You may be surprised at what polite, sophisticated people do at the table. Finally, the timing of meals varies from country to country. Let me illustrate some of these points.

During his military career, a friend of mine—a very finicky eater—was assigned to the diplomatic corps. In that capacity, he attended a state dinner in Saudi Arabia. The first plate presented at the meal was a bare plate with a goat's eyeball sitting on it. My friend could not refuse to eat it and cause an international incident. He grabbed his chest and fell over backward in his chair, faking a heart attack. They carried him out of the room, and the meal continued.

I tend to be a bit more daring in my culinary pursuits. Some of the best and most enjoyable eating experiences I have had have been in places like Indonesia, China, and Spain. On one occasion, I stayed in Tianjin, China, at a government guest house for 10 days. During that time, every meal was Chinese, and no dish was served more than once. The taste of the food and the presentation of the dishes were exquisite. There were small boiled shrimp arranged in the shape of a crab; there were beets carved in the shape of a rose; there were clumps of cabbage laid out in the shape of a forest.

I asked my host if I could see the kitchen, and he obliged. The room was elegant in its simplicity. The walls all had cabinets that were waist high and about 30 inches deep. About every 10 feet, there was a 15-inch hole in the countertop. Underneath the hole was a steel-lined box in which wood fires were built. A wok dish was the only cooking vessel, and a knife and some chopsticks were the only utensils. I was amazed at the quality and variety of food that came from that simple room.

In many Asian cultures, what we consider bad manners are, in fact, very acceptable. People usually serve themselves from common serving dishes. The more formal eaters use the opposite end of their chopsticks when diving into the common dish. Elbows on the table are the norm. There is a lot of noise at the table. One time I asked a Japanese friend to dinner at my house. My wife had prepared an excellent American meal, complete with soup. When my friend picked up the bowl and slurped loudly, my wife was amazed. I explained that this was a way for our guest to show how much he liked the soup. The louder he slurped, the more he enjoyed it.

During one of my very first trips to France, my host took me to a restaurant for dinner. I was afraid to try sweetbreads or goat's brain or raw meat and so, when he suggested a dish that was a half-chicken, I jumped at the opportunity. The problem was that it was a half-chicken—half of the body, half of the head and one foot still attached to a leg.

I draw the line at Indian food. I don't like curry and have yet to taste an Indian food dish that I like. During a five-day trip to India, I was able to avoid the inevitable. Because I was with a different host each day, when asked what I would like to eat, I simply replied, "Let's try Chinese today."

In Europe, dinners tend to start late. In France, the earliest you begin dinner is 7 p.m., and 8 or 9 is more normal. In Spain or Italy, 10 o'clock is the usual starting time. In most of Asia, dinnertime is around 7 p.m. In Japan, meals tend to start a little earlier—say, 6:30 or so —because the Japanese want either to go back to work or to begin the two-hour commute home.

Here are some suggestions you can apply to your eating adventures:

- Be flexible.

- Try at least a little bit of each dish presented to you.

- If you don't want to know what it is, don't ask. Just taste it.

- Slice the mystery meat thinly and swallow it whole so you don't have to taste it.

- Think pleasant thoughts, and don't concentrate on what you are eating.

- Be prepared to be pleasantly surprised.

EMERGENCIES

Sometimes you are confronted with unpleasant experiences during your travels. For example, what do you do if you get sick? Most hotels have clinics or doctors on call. You should be able to get medical attention fairly quickly. I had an interesting experience during a trip to Hong Kong. As the plane was clearing 10,000 feet at the beginning of the 15-hour nonstop flight, I realized that I had an ear infection. It was not a great flight.

When I arrived at the hotel, I called the doctor. A Chinese doctor came to my room, a small man who weighed about 90 pounds. He confirmed that I had an ear infection, gave me a shot of penicillin, and left me some pills. He said to come to the clinic if there was no improvement in two days. There wasn't. I went to the clinic to find that the doctor who originally saw me wasn't in. His American partner was.

I explained the problem. The American doctor sighed and said: "I can't get my Chinese partner to prescribe the right amount of medicine for people of your size." I weigh about 250 pounds and had been given enough medicine for someone who weighs about 100 pounds. The American doctor gave me the right dosage of penicillin and, in two days, the infection was gone.

There will be times when you are confronted with situations that put you in danger. We are used to personal crime in our cities and know how to avoid it most of the time. In most foreign cities you will visit, crime isn't so much of a problem. You can walk down the darkest alley in Tokyo and not be afraid. There are times, however, when political situations will place you in danger.

In 1978, during a trip to Paris, Harold O'Kelley, the then-chairman of Datapoint Corporation, and I were walking down the Boulevard Houssman, where there are many stores and shops and banks. We were walking past one of the banks when I noticed a group of people with ski masks just beside us. It was in the middle of June and hot. All of a sudden, they took out crowbars, smashed the plate glass windows, and threw firebombs into the bank. Harold and I agreed to watch from the other side of the street.

During the drug wars in Colombia, I had occasion to hold a dealer meeting there. The normal place to meet would have been Bogotá. But there were several killings and acts of terrorism in that city. It turned out that President Bush was meeting with the presidents of Colombia, Bolivia, and Peru in Cartagena. So I moved the dealer meeting to that beautiful city. With all the added security to protect the presidents, our meeting went off without incident.

The U.S. Department of State has a current list of hot spots around the world and publishes travel advisories to help you know where there are dangerous situations. Check with them before you go on your trip. With a little experience, you will learn where the trouble spots are and how to avoid them.

GIFTS

I am sure you have heard that many people doing business internationally often give and receive gifts. You will get many different opinions about gift giving. At the end of the day, you have to reach your own conclusion and do what is right for you.

Many international visitors will bring gifts to their American hosts. Usually, these are something from the home country—a souvenir. You should receive them politely. Don't open the gift unless you are invited to do so by the giver. When you travel, you may want to take along some souvenirs as well. It is okay to have your company logo on the gift as long as it is discreet and tasteful.

The real problem with gifts is the cost. There are several facets to this issue. For example, if you are visiting an official of a foreign government, it is not a good idea to give him a diamond wristwatch for his wife or the keys to a car. Remember the Foreign Corrupt Practices Act.

All countries, however, do not have a law like the FCPA. During one of my visits to an equatorial country, my distributor had a very large package to give to the person we were visiting. It was a fur coat. I asked what anyone could do with a fur coat in 90-degree heat. He told me it was to be used by the wife of the official on their trip to Europe, which he, the distributor, had given them.

These situations are rare. The more common problem comes up when you bring a gift to your host and then, when he visits you, he brings a gift. It may be a little more expensive than the one you brought so that he can show you respect. You bring another gift on your next visit. However innocent the start, a situation like this can snowball and get out of control.

I have avoided bringing gifts unless I am personally very close to the host. Then, it is on a very personal basis, and you can give a gift in the same way we share gifts here.

If you decide you want to give gifts, there are a few things to consider.

- Make sure the gift is not too valuable and yet not so inexpensive as to be insulting.

- It is not necessary to wrap the gift, except in Japan. There you wrap it in softly colored nonwhite paper with no ribbon.

- Put your company logo or business card discreetly on the gift or box.

- Don't make a big scene about giving or receiving the gift.

- Be sensitive to local customs. Don't take liquor to an Arab country, for example.

TIPPING

In the United States, we expect to tip people for services rendered. In fact, the providers of service expect it as well. In New York, a waiter came running out of a restaurant after me. The service had been lousy and I had left no tip. When he demanded a tip, I said: "Get another job. That's the only tip you'll get from me!"

In most situations, you will know how to act with regard to tipping. There are just a few cautions. In Europe, tip the taxi driver but, before you tip the waiter, ask if service is included in the bill—it usually is. If you are especially impressed with the quality of service, just leave a nominal amount of cash on the table as you leave. In many countries, tipping is not expected or even allowed. In Japan, people provide good service because they like their job and want to do what they are supposed to do. In China, it is an insult to tip a taxi driver.

You will be confused when dealing in different currencies, particularly when it comes to tipping. You usually tip someone instinctively and quickly, without a lot of time to calculate the U.S. dollar equivalent of the tip. You tip as you are paying the taxi driver and as the bellhop drops your luggage in your hotel room. After a visit to Japan, where 100 yen was, at the time, worth about 50 cents, I made a bellhop in Hong Kong very happy. I gave him 100 Hong Kong dollars for carrying one bag. That was a U.S. $15 tip. He was smiling as he left my room.

Before you travel to any country, find out what the local custom is.

EXPECT THE UNEXPECTED

Whenever you travel or receive foreign visitors, be prepared to be surprised. If you are not flexible and sensitive to local customs, you will be less successful than if you are. Some very bizarre things will happen to you. You will need to react in a way that doesn't leave a bad impression. You will need patience.

On my first trip to the People's Republic of China in 1984, I arrived at the Great Wall Hotel in Beijing. This was a brand-new hotel, which had opened two weeks before my visit. I arrived at the registration desk and found that they did, indeed, have a reservation for me. I handed the clerk my credit card. She said that they didn't take credit cards. So I took out traveler's checks. She said they didn't take traveler's checks but directed me to another desk where I could cash the checks. At that desk, they said they would be happy to cash the checks and asked my room number. I told them I didn't have a room in the hotel yet. They would not cash the checks without a room number. It took 30 minutes to resolve the situation—after I had traveled over 20 hours just to get there! That takes a lot of patience and flexibility.

You can see that the world is not the same all over; there are many differences. Don't be intimidated by the differences, however. You should recognize the differences in countries and cultures but focus on the similarities. If you want more information of the kind presented here, buy Roger Axtell's book called *Do's and Taboos*

Around the World. It is a wonderfully written book in its third printing. You will find it very useful in helping you cope with some of the issues I have described here.

In the next chapter, we look at the conclusion of this journey and the beginning of your international adventure.

13 | ❧

The Beginning

Now the real fun begins. You have considered all the implications of doing business internationally. You have made the commitment to go for it. You have the agreement of your colleagues. Now you get to execute the plan. This is the real beginning.

Just before you jump out of the airplane, however, let's make sure the parachute works. There are a few things I would like to remind you of and a few more suggestions I would like to make.

The two key issues with which I began this book are technology and change. We live in a high-tech world today, and it is incumbent on us to make the most effective use of that technology. Throughout the book, I have offered some suggestions about what technology can do for you with respect to the topic being covered.

On an ongoing basis, you need to keep in touch with

what is available in the IT world that will have application to what you do. Be prepared to adapt to new situations and new processes. Be ready to change.

That leads to the second theme of this book—change. We have talked about change and the difference attitude can have on the way change impacts your business. Don't resist change. Don't just accept it either. Embrace it. That does not mean to change just for the sake of changing. It is a call to action, however, to get you thinking outside the box.

Understand your opportunities and challenges before you start. Do the right amount of research. Make sure the team is signed up to support the effort. Set your targets high but realistically.

The four P's of marketing are product, place, promotion, and pricing, and all your experience in conducting business in the United States will apply to your international business as well. But there are differences that you and your team must consider as you proceed. Think about the market requirements. Think about the impact language differences will have. Consider the effect that time and distance will have on communications, both internally and externally.

You will certainly make adjustments in the financial model of your company. If you do things right, you will see positive impact on both revenue and profit. However, you need to be aware of the shifting of money among the various lines of the P & L between revenue and profit. Expect surprises and bring lots of money. An investment is required, and that investment will be large relative to your business.

You might have noticed that my favorite subject is people. Meeting and working with people from all over the world is what makes an international job so much fun and so rewarding. Otherwise, no one would put up with the pain and suffering that comes with all the odd hours and all the travel. Dealing with people from different cultures and backgrounds provides endless opportunity to expand your mind and your experiences.

The whirlwind world tour provided in the preceding chapter gives you the flavor of what you might expect when you work in the international arena. In fairly short order, you will build a library of stories and experiences that will make your life richer.

In parting, let me offer a few guidelines you can take with you as you travel around the world.

- Look for alternatives. There is always another way.

- Be aggressive but not foolish. Windows open and close quickly.

- Obey the law—follow the rules. The consequences of not doing so are dire.

- Be flexible. You will find that the world is not the same all over.

APPENDIX A

International Standards and Testing Agencies

Here is a list of standards agencies around the world. The addresses and phone numbers should help you contact them for specific information about agency approvals in their country.

Country & Mark	Standards Agency	Testing and/or Certification Agency
Argentina	IRAM—Instituto Argentino de Recionalization de Materiales Chile 1192 C. Postal 1098 Buenos Aires ARGENTINA Telephone: (54) 1 37 37 51	INTI—Instituto Nacional de Tecnologia Industrial LN Alem No. 1067 1001 Buenos Aires ARGENTINA Telex: 21859 INTI AR
Australia	SAA—Standards Association of Australia (NCB) 80 Arthur Street P.O. Box 458 North Sydney, New South Wales 2059 AUSTRALIA Telephone: (61) 2 963 4111 FAX: (61) 2 959 3896 Telex: 99-26514 astan	SECV—State Electrical Commission of Victoria 15 William Street Melbourne, Victoria 3000 AUSTRALIA Telephone: (61) 3 392 2253 Telex: 31153

Country & Mark	Standards Agency	Testing and/or Certification Agency
Australia (cont.)		Sydney County Council Test. Labs 14 Nelson Street Chatswood, New South Wales AUSTRALIA Telephone: (61) 02 410511 Telex: 22810
		EANSW—Energy Authority of New South Wales 1 Castlereagh Street Box 485, GPO Sydney, New South Wales 2001 AUSTRALIA Telephone: (61) 2 234 4444 FAX: (61) 2 221 6229 TELEX: NSWEA AA170320
		ETSA—Electricity Trust of South Australia 26–56 Burbridge Road Mile End, South Australia 5031 AUSTRALIA Telephone: (61) 08 352 0719 Telex: 88655
		SECQ—State Electricity Commission of Queensland GPO Box 10 Brisbane, Queensland 4001 AUSTRALIA

Country & Mark	Standards Agency	Testing and/or Certification Agency
Australia (cont.)		SECWA—State Energy Commission of Western Australia GPO Box L921 Perth, Western Australia AUSTRALIA Telephone: (61) 09 277 2488 Telex: 92674
Austria	ÖVE—Österreichischer Verband für Elektrotechnik (NCB) Eschenbachgasse 9 A-1010 Wien AUSTRIA Telephone: (43) 1 587 63 73 FAX: (43) 1 567 408	
Belgium	CEB—Comité Electrotechnique Belge B-Brussels BELGIUM Telephone: (32) 2 512 0028 FAX: (32) 2 511 2938	CEBEC—Comité Electrotechnique Belge Service (NCB) Rodestraat 125 B-1630 Linkebeek BELGIUM Telephone: (32) 2 380 85 20 FAX: (32) 2 380 61 33 Telex: 62834 (CEBEC B)
Brazil	ABNT—Associacão Brasileira de Normas Tecnicas Rua Marquês de ITU 88-4° Andar 01223 São Paulo, SP BRAZIL Telephone: (55) 11 35 94 33 Telex: 112 1452 CELB BR	SINMETRO—National System of Metrology Standardization and Industrial Quality

Country & Mark	Standards Agency	Testing and/or Certification Agency
Bulgaria	State Commission Science & Technical Programs Standards Office 21, 6th September Street Sofia 1000 BULGARIA Telephone: 85 91 Telex: 22570 DKS BG	
Canada	CSA—Canadian Standards Association (NCB) 178 Rexdale Blvd. Rexdale (Toronto) Ontario M9W 1R3 CANADA Telephone: (416) 747-4000 or 747-4007 Telephone/CB: (416) 747-4236 Main FAX: (416) 747-4149 Central Canada Operations (same address as above) Telephone: (416) 747-4007 FAX: (416) 747-2475	Other CSA offices: 865 Ellington Street Pointe-Claire (Montréal) PQ H9R 5E8 Telephone: (514) 694-8110 FAX: (514) 694-5001 40 Rooney Crest Moncton, NB E1E 4M3 Telephone: (506) 858-9300 FAX: (506) 858-9302 50 Paramount Road Winnipeg, MB R2X 2W3 Telephone: (204) 632-6633 FAX: (204) 632-1796 13799 Commerce Parkway Richmond (Vancouver) BC V6V 2N9 Telephone: (604) 273-4581 FAX: (604) 273-5815 1707–94th Street Edmonton, AB T6N 1E6 Telephone: (403) 450-2111 FAX: (403) 461-5322

Country & Mark	Standards Agency	Testing and/or Certification Agency
China, People's Republic of	CSBS—China State Bureau for Standardization P.O. Box 820 Beijing PEOPLE'S REPUBLIC OF CHINA Telegrams: 0621 Beijing	CCEE—China Commission for Conformity Certification of Electrical Equipment (NCB) 2 Shoudu Tiyuguan Nanlu 100044 Beijing PEOPLE'S REPUBLIC OF CHINA Telephone: (86) 1 832 00 88; Ext. for CB: 2659 FAX: (86) 1 832 08 25 Telex: 222295 (RIMST CN)
Czechoslovakia	Urad pro Normalizacia Mereni (Office for Standards and Measurements) Václavské nam. 19 113 47 Praha 1 CZECHOSLOVAKIA Telephone: (42) 2 26 22 51 FAX: (42) 2 265 795 Telex: 12948 UNM	Elektrotechnicky zkusebni ustav (NCB) Post Office 71 CS-171 02 Praha 8–Troja CZECHOSLOVAKIA Telephone: (42) 2 84 0641 FAX: (42) 2 84 00 84 Telex: 122880 (EZU C)
Denmark	DEK—Dansk Elektroteknisk Komite (Danish Electrotechnical Committee) Strandgade 36 DK-1401 Copenhagen K DENMARK Attn: DANELKOMITE Telephone: (01) 57 50 50 Telex: FOTEX DK 16600 FAX: 011-45-1576350	DEMKO (NCB) Lyskaer 8, Postbox 514 DK-2730 Herlev DENMARK Telephone: (45) 44 94 72 66 FAX: (45) 44 94 7261 Telex: 35125 (DEMKO DK)

Country & Mark	Standards Agency	Testing and/or Certification Agency
Egypt	EOS—Egyptian Organization for Standardization & Quality Control 2 Latin America Street Garden City, Cairo EGYPT Telephone: (20) 29720 Telex: 93296 EOS UN	
Finland	SETI—Electrical Inspectorate Sarkiniementie 3 P.O. Box 21 SF-00210 Helsinki 21 FINLAND Telephone: (358) 0-69631 FAX: (358) 0-69254 74 Telex: 122877 SETI SF	
France	UTE—Union Technique de l'Électricité (NCB) Cedex 64 F-92052 Paris la Défense FRANCE Telephone: (33) 1 46 91 11 11 FAX: (33) 1 47 89 45 87 Telex: 620816 (CEFUTE F)	LCIE—Laboratorie Central des Industries Électriques 33, Avenue du Général Leclerc P.B. 8 F-92260 Fontenay aux Roses FRANCE Telephone: (33) 1 40 95 60 60 Telex: 250080 f FAX: (33) 1 40 95 60 95
Germany	DKE—Deutsche Elektrotechnische Kommission im DIN und VDE (German Electrotechnical Commission of DIN and VDE) Stresemannallee 15 D-6000 Frankfurt 70 GERMANY Telephone: (49) 69 6308 0 FAX: (49) 69 6308 273 Telex: 2-12871	VDE (NCB)— VDE-Prüf und Zertifierungsinstitut Merianstrasse 28 D-6050 Offenbach am Main GERMANY Telephone: (49) 69 83 06 222 FAX: (49) 69 83 06 555 Telex: 4152796 VDEP D

Country & Mark	Standards Agency	Testing and/or Certification Agency
Germany (cont.)		TUV-Technischer Überwachungs-Verein Albionstrasse 56 D-1000 Berlin GERMANY Telephone: (49) 30 75 3021 Telex: 1 84 517

TUV Essen
6 Brighton Road
Clifton, NY 07012-1647
Telephone:
(201) 773-8880
FAX: (201) 773-8834
West Coast: Palo Alto,
CA
Telephone:
(415) 961-0521
FAX: (415) 961-9119

TUV Rheinland of
North America
(Headquarters)
12 Commerce Road
Newtown, CT 06470
Telephone:
(203) 426-0888
FAX/Engineering:
(203) 270-8883
FAX/Administration:
(203) 426-3156

Other offices of TUV:
Rheinland/North
America, Inc.
Pleasanton, CA
Telephone:
(510) 734-8100
FAX: (510) 734-8455

San Diego, CA
Telephone:
(619) 792-2770
FAX: (619) 792-2774

Austin, TX
Telephone:
(512) 343-6231
FAX: (512) 343-6233

Country & Mark	Standards Agency	Testing and/or Certification Agency
Germany (cont.)		Glenview, IL Telephone: (708) 699-0310 FAX: (708) 699-6898

Portland, OR
Telephone:
(503) 620-0418
FAX: (503) 620-6490

Marlborough, MA
Telephone:
(508) 460-0792
FAX: (508) 460-9073

Longwood, FL
Telephone:
(407) 774-1222
FAX: (407) 774-1033

Livonia, MI
Telephone:
(313) 464-8881
FAX: (313) 464-8919

Canada (Ontario)
Telephone:
(416) 733-3677
FAX: (416) 733-7781

LGA—
(Landesgewerbeanstalt
Bayem)
Gewerbemuseums-
platz 2
D-8500 Nürnberg 1
GERMANY
Telephone:
(49) 911 20 17 336
FAX: (49) 911 22 47 74

U.S. Representative
(Massachusetts):
Telephone:
(508) 526-1687
FAX: (508) 526-7718

Country & Mark	Standards Agency	Testing and/or Certification Agency
Greece	ELOT—The Hellenic Organization of Standardization (NCB) 313, Acharnon Street GR-111 45 Athens GREECE Telephone: (30) 1 201 50 25 FAX: (30) 1 202 07 76 or (30) 1 202 59 17 Telex: 219621 or 219670 (ELOT GR)	
Hong Kong	Hong Kong Standards & Testing Centre 10 Dai Wang St. Taipo Industrial Estate Taipo, N.T. HONG KONG Telephone: (852) 667 00 21 FAX: (852) 664 43 53 Telex: 54652 (STDS HX)	
Hungary	MSZH—Magyar Szabvanyugi Hivatal (Hungarian Office for Standardization) Pf. 24 H-1450 Budapest 9 HUNGARY Telephone: (36) 183-011 Telex: 225723 NORM H	MEEI—Magyar Elektrotechnikai Ellenorzo Intezet (NCB) (Hungarian Institute for Testing Electrical Equipment) Vácí út 48/a-b Pf. 441 H-1395 Budapest XIII HUNGARY Telephone: (36) 1 49 55 61 FAX: (36) 1 129 06 84 Telex: 224931 (MEEI H)

Country & Mark	Standards Agency	Testing and/or Certification Agency
Iceland	RER—Rafmagnesftirlit Riskisins (NCB) (The State Electrical Inspection) Pósthólf 8240 IS-128 Reykjavik ICELAND Telephone: (354) 1 814133 FAX: (354) 1 689256	
India	BIS—Bureau of Indian Standards "Manak Bhavan" 9 Bahadur Shah Zafar Mrg. New Delhi 110002 INDIA Telephone: (91) 11 266021/270131 Telex: 031-3970 ISI/ND	
Indonesia	Badan Kerjasama Standardisasi LIPI–YDNI (LIPI–YDNI Joint Standardization Committee) Jalan Teuku Chiek Ditiro 43 P.O. Box 250 Jakarta INDONESIA Telephone: (62) 351658	
Iran	Institute of Standards and Industrial Research of Iran P. O. Box 2937 Tehran Iran Telephone: (98) 2221 6031-8	

Country & Mark	Standards Agency	Testing and/or Certification Agency
Ireland	NSAI—National Standards Authority of Ireland (NCB) EOLAS, The Irish Science & Technical Agency (NCB) Glasnevin IRL—Dublin 9 IRELAND Telephone: (353) 1 37 01 01 FAX: (353) 1 36 98 21 Telex: 32501 (IIRS EI)	NETH—National Electrical Test House Ballymun Road IRL—Dublin 9 IRELAND Telephone: (353) 1 370 101 FAX: (353) 1 379 620 Telex: 32502 OLASEI

NASI of America 5 Medallion Center (Greeley St.) Merrimack, NH 03054 Telephone: (603) 424-7070 FAX: (603) 429-1427 |
| **Israel** | SII—Standards Institution of Israel (NCB) 42 Chaim Levenon Street IL-Tel Aviv 69977 ISRAEL Telephone: (972) 3 545 41 71 FAX: (972) 3 541 56 54 Telex: 35508 (SIIT IL) | |
| **Italy** | CEI—Comitato Elettrotecnico Italiano (Italian Electrotechnical Committee) Viale Monza 259 I-20126 Milano ITALY Telephone: (39) 2 25 50 641 Telex: 312207 CEITAL 1 | IMQ (NCB)—Instituto Italiano del Marchio di Qualitá Via Quintiliano, 43 I-20138 Milano ITALY Telephone: (39) 2 5073 1 FAX: (39) 2 5073 271 Telex: 310494 (IMQ I) |

Country & Mark	Standards Agency	Testing and/or Certification Agency
Japan	All certification and test agencies are part of "MITI"—The Ministry of International Trade and Industry	JET—Japan Electrical Testing Laboratory 5-14-12 Yoyogi Shibuya-ku, Tokyo 151 JAPAN Telephone: (81) 3 466-5121 FAX: (81) 3 468-9090
	Apply for Dentori approvals at JIS— Japanese Industrial Standards Office, Agency of Industrial Science & Technology 1-3-1 Kasumigaseki 1-Chome Chiyoda-ku, Tokyo 100 JAPAN Telephone: (81) 3 501-9296 FAX: (81) 3 580-1418	IECEE Council of Japan (NCB) c/o JMI Institute 9-15, Akasaka 1-chome, Minato-ku Tokyo JAPAN Telephone: (81) 3 3583 4136 FAX: (81) 3 3583 4137
	UL has information on MITI requirements. Contact: UL Overseas Inspection Services 1285 Walt Whitman Road Melville, NY 11747 Telephone: (516) 271-6200 FAX: (516) 271-8250	Electrical Appliance Safety Office (same address as JIS) Telephone: (81) 3 501-1511 FAX: (81) 3 501 1836
Korea, Democratic People's Republic of (North)	Committee for Standardization Sosong guyok Ryonmod dong Pyongyang DEMOCRATIC PEOPLE'S REPUBLIC OF KOREA Telephone: 3327	

Country & Mark	Standards Agency	Testing and/or Certification Agency
Korea, Republic of (South)	Industrial Advancement Administration 94-267 Yongdeungpo-Dong Yongdeungpo-Ku Seoul REPUBLIC OF KOREA Telephone: (82) 2 633-8815	IECEE Council of Korea (NCB) KAITECH—Korea Academy of Industrial Technology 222-13, Guru-Dong, Guro-ku 152-650 Seoul REPUBLIC OF KOREA Telephone: (82) 2 860 1453 FAX: (82) 2 860 1465 Telex: K28456 (FINCEN)
Luxembourg	ITM 26, Zithe Bte Postale 26 L-2010 LUXEMBOURG Telephone: (352) 49 921 2106 FAX: (352) 49 14 47 Telex: 2985 MINIES	
Mexico	DGN—Dirección General de Normas Secretaria de Patrimonio y Fomento Industrial Puente de Tecamachalco No. 6, Lomas de Tecamachalco Sección Fuentes Naucalpan de Juárez ESTADO DE MEXICO, C.P. 53950 Telephone: (520) 395-36-43 Telex: 1775690	

Country & Mark	Standards Agency	Testing and/or Certification Agency
Netherlands	NEC—Nederlands Elektrotechnisch Comite Kalfieslaan 2 Postbus 5059 2600 GB Delft THE NETHERLANDS Telephone: (31) 15 69 03 90 FAX: (31) 15 69 01 90 Telex: 38144 NNI NL	N.V.KEMA—Nv tot Keuring van Elktrotechnische Materialen (NCB) Utrechseweg 310 Postbus 9035 NL-6800 ET Arnhem THE NETHERLANDS Telephone: (31) 85 56 28 15 FAX: (31) 85 51 49 22 Telex: 75132 (KLTI NL)
New Zealand	SANZ—Standards Association of New Zealand 181–187 Victoria Street (Mail: Private Bag) Wellington 1 NEW ZEALAND Telephone: (64) 04 384 2108 FAX: (64) 04 384 3938 Telex: 3850 SANZ NZ	
Norway	NEK—Norsk Elektroteknisk Komite (Norwegian Electrotechnical Committee) Oscarsgate 20 P.O. Box 7099 Homansbyen Oslo 3 NORWAY Telephone: (47) 2 606 697 Telex: 17206 NENEKN	NEMKO (NCB) Norges Elektriske Materiellkontroll Gaustadalleen 30 Postboks 73 Blindern N-0314 Oslo 3 NORWAY Telephone: (47) 2 69 19 50 FAX: (47) 2 69 86 36 Telex: 181288 (NEMKO N)
Pakistan	Pakistan Standards Institution 39 Garden Road Saddar, Karachi 3 PAKISTAN Telephone: (92) 73088	

Country & Mark	Standards Agency	Testing and/or Certification Agency
Poland	Polski Komitet Normalizacji Miar i Jakosci Polish (Committee for Standardization, Measures and Quality Control) ul. Elektoralna 2 00-139 Warsaw POLAND	CBJW—Central Office for Product Quality (NCB) ul. Swietojerska 14B PL-00-050 Warszawa POLAND Telephone: (48) 22 27 70 71 or (48) 22 26 67 65 FAX: (48) 22 26 67 65 Telex: 816196 (ZNAK PL)
		Association of Polish Electrical Engineers, Quality Testing Office ul. Wsopolna 32/46 Warsaw POLAND Telephone: (48) 22 21 90 38
Portugal	CEP—Commissão Electrotécnica Portuguesa Rua Infantaria 16, n°41-2° 1200 Lisbon PORTUGAL Telephone: (351) 681048-681049	IPQ—Instituto Portugués da Qualidade (NCB) Rua José Estevão, 83A P-1199-Lisboa Codex PORTUGAL Telephone: (351) 1 52 37 55 FAX: (351) 1 53 00 33 Telex: 13042 (QUALIT P)
Romania	Institutul Roman de Standardizare (Romanian Standards Institute) Bucaresti, Sect. 1 str. Roma 32-34 R71219-RS ROMANIA Telephone: (40) 337660 Telex: 011312	

Country & Mark	Standards Agency	Testing and/or Certification Agency
Russian Federation	VNIIS (NCB) Electrichesky 3 Moscow 123856 Telephone: (7) 095 253 70 06 Telex: 411378 (GOST SU)	

Saudi Arabia	SASO—Saudi Arabian
	  Standards
	  Organization
	Sitteen Street
	P.O. Box 3437
	Riyadh 11471
	KINGDOM OF SAUDI
	  ARABIA
	Telephone:
	(966) 1 479 0406
	FAX: (966) 1 479 3063
	Telex: 401610 SASO SJ	

Singapore	Singapore Institute of
	  Standards and
	  Industrial Research
	1 Science Park Drive
	Singapore 0511
	REPUBLIC OF
	  SINGAPORE
	Telephone: (65) 778 7777
	Telex: RS 28499 SISIR
	FAX: (65) 778 0086
		Postal address:
		P.O. Box 1128
		Singapore 9111

South Africa	SABS–South Africa
	  Bureau of Standards
	Private Bag X191
	Pretoria 0001
	REPUBLIC OF SOUTH
	  AFRICA
	Telephone:
	(012) 428-7911
	Telex: 3626 SA	

Country & Mark	Standards Agency	Testing and/or Certification Agency
Spain	IRANOR—Instituto Nacional de Racionalización y Normalización Zurbano 46 Madrid 10 SPAIN Telephone: (34) 410 46 76 Telex: 46545 UNOR E	AEE (NCB) Asociación Electrotécnica y Electronica Española Francisco Gervas 3 E-28020 Madrid SPAIN Telephone: (34) 1 616 00 18 FAX: (34) 1 616 23 72 Telex: 48476 (IAAS E)
Sweden	SEK—Svenska Elektriska Kommissionen (Swedish Electrotechnical Commission) Kistagängen 19 Box 1284 S-164 28 Kista-Stockholm SWEDEN Telephone: (46) 8 750 78 20 FAX: (46) 8 751 84 70 Telex: 8126725 SEKELNORM S	SEMKO—Svenska Elektriska Materielkontrollanstalten AB (NCB) (Swedish Institute for Testing & Approval of Electrical Equipment) Torshamnsgatan 43 Box 1103 S-164 22 Kista-Stockholm SWEDEN Telephone: (46) 8 750 00 00 FAX: (46) 8 750 60 30 Telex: 8126010 (SEMKO S)
Switzerland	SEV—Schweizerischer Elektrotechnischer Verein (NCB) Prüfstelle Zürich (P-ZH) Postfach CH-8034 Zürich SWITZERLAND (for parcels: Seefeldstrasse 301 CH-8008 Zürich) Telephone: (41) 1 384 91 11 FAX: (41) 1 551426 Telex: 81 74 31 (SEV CH)	

Country & Mark	Standards Agency	Testing and/or Certification Agency
Taiwan	BCIQ—Bureau of Commodity Inspection and Quarantine, Ministry of Economic Affairs, Republic of China 4, Section 1, Chinan Road Taipei TAIWAN ROC Telephone: (886) 2 351-2141 FAX: (886) 2 393-2324 Telex: 27247 BCIQ	

United Kingdom	British Electrotechnical Committee (NCB), British Standards Institution
	2 Park Street
	London W1A 2BS
	ENGLAND
	Telephone:
	  (44) 71 629 90 00
	FAX: (44) 71 629 05 06
	Telex: 266933
	  (BSILON G)
		BSI—Quality Assurance, Certification & Assessment Department (NCB)
		P.O. Box 375
		Milton Keynes MK14 6LL
		ENGLAND
		Telephone:
		  (44) 908 22 09 08
		FAX: (44) 908 22 06 71
		Telex: 827682
		  (BSI QAS G)
		
		BEAB—British Electrotechnical Approvals Board (NCB)
		Mark House, The Green
		9/11 Queen's Road
		Hersham,
		  Walton-on-Thames
		Surrey KT12 5NA
		ENGLAND
		Telephone:
		  (44) 932 24 44 01
		FAX: (44) 932 22 66 03
		Telex: 8812027
		  (BEAB G)

Country & Mark	Standards Agency	Testing and/or Certification Agency
United Kingdom (cont.)		BASEC—British Approvals Service for Electric Cables P.O. Box 390 Milton Keynes GM-MK14 6LN ENGLAND Telephone: (44) 908 31 55 55 FAX: (44) 908 32 08 56 Telex: 82682 BSIQAS G
		BASEEFA—British Approval Services/ Electronic Equipment for Flammable Atmosphere Health & Safety, Executive Harpur Hill, Buxton Derbyshire ENGLAND Telephone: 0298 (Std. Code: 6211)
		ASTA—Association of Short Circuit Testing Authorities, Inc. (NCB) Prudential Chambers 23/24 Market Place Rugby CV21 3DU ENGLAND Telephone: (44) 788 578 435 FAX: (44) 788 573 605 Telex: 311794 (CHACOM G)
United States of America	ANSI—American National Standards Institute 11 W. 42 Street New York, NY 10036 Telephone: (212) 642-4900	ARL—Applied Research Labs of Florida 5371 NW 161 Street Miami, FL 33014 Telephone: (305) 624-4800 FAX: (305) 624-3652

Country & Mark	Standards Agency	Testing and/or Certification Agency
United States of America (cont.)	FAX/Sales: (212) 302-1286 Main FAX: (212) 398-0023 NEMA—National Electrical Manufacturers Association Suite 300 2101 L Street, NW Washington, DC 20037 Telephone: (202) 457-8400 FAX: (202) 457-8411 NFPA—National Fire Protection Agency 1 Battery March Park Quincy, MA 02269	DS&G—Dash, Straus & Goodhue 593 Massachusetts Avenue Boxborough, MA 01719 Telephone: (508) 263-2662 FAX: (508) 263-7086 Telex: 317-632-DASH ETL—ETL Testing Labs, Inc. Industrial Park Cortland, NY 13045 Telephone: (607) 753-6711; (800) 354-3851 FAX: (607) 756-9891 Other ETL Offices: NY Metro 195 Anderson Ave. Moonachie, NJ 07074 Telephone: (201) 939-8085 FAX: (201) 939-3192 660 Forbes Road, So. San Francisco, CA 94084 Telephone: (415) 871-1414 FAX: (415) 873-7357 5855-P Oakbrook Parkway Norcross, GA 30093 Phone: (404) 446-7294 FAX: (404) 446-7025 Factory Mutual Insurance Co. 1151 Boston-Providence Highway Norwood, MA 02062 Telephone: (617) 769-7900 Telex: 92-4415

Country & Mark	Standards Agency	Testing and/or Certification Agency
United States of America (cont.)		MET—MET Electrical Testing Co. 916 W. Patapsco Avenue Baltimore, MD 21230 Telephone: (301) 354-2200 FAX: (301) 354-1624
		UL—Underwriters Laboratories, Inc. (NCB) 333 Pfingsten Road Northbrook, IL 60062 Telephone: (708) 272-8800 FAX: (708) 272-8129 Telex: 6502543343
		Other UL Offices: 1655 Scott Blvd. Santa Clara, CA 95050 Telephone: (408) 985-2400 FAX: (408) 296-3256 Telex: 470607
		1285 Walt Whitman Road Melville, Long Island, NY 11747 Telephone: (516) 271-6200 FAX: (516) 271-8259 Telex: 6852015
		12 Laboratory Drive P.O. Box 13995 Research Triangle Park, NC 27709 Telephone: (919) 549-1400 FAX: (919) 549-1842 Telex: 4937928

Country & Mark	Standards Agency	Testing and/or Certification Agency
Venezuela	CODELECTRA en Conjunto con COVENIN Avda. Ppal. Las Mercedes-Edf. Centro Victorial Piso 1 Caracas 1060 VENEZUELA Telephone: (58) 91 99 06	COVENIN—Ppal. Comis. Venezolana de Normas Industriales Av. Boyaca (COTA MIL) Edf. Fundación La Salle 5° Piso Caracas 105 VENEZUELA
International	IECEE-CTL Secretariat Särkiniementie 3 P.O. Box 21 SF-00211 Helsinki 21 FINLAND Telephone: (358) 0 696 31 FAX: (358) 0 676 986 Telex: 122887 (SETI SF) IECEE c/o Central Office of the IEC P.O. Box 131 3, rue de Varembé CH-1211 Geneva 20 SWITZERLAND Telephone: (41) 22 734 01 50 Telex: 414121 (LEC CH)	

APPENDIX B

Listing of Country Desk Officers, U.S. Department of Commerce

This is the current list of country desk officers at the U.S. Department of Commerce. They are very obliging in answering your questions. To call a desk officer, dial area code 202, followed by the phone number listed (482 + the number of the direct line). To write, address your letter to the appropriate officer at his or her room number, followed by U.S. Department of Commerce, Washington, DC 20230. The names of the officers change frequently. I have found that, when the person I called is no longer at that specific desk, the person answering the phone was able to lead me in the right direction to get to the appropriate officer.

Country	Desk Officer	Direct Dial Phone (202) 482-	Room
A			
Afghanistan	Timothy Gilman	2954	2308
Albania	Lynn Fabrizio	4915	3413
Algeria	Christopher Cerone/	1860	2029B
	Claude Clement	5545	2033
Angola	Finn Holm-Olsen	4228	3321
Anguilla	Michelle Brooks	2527	2039
Antigua and Barbuda	Michelle Brooks	2527	2039
Argentina	Randy Mye	1548	3021
Aruba	Michelle Brooks	2527	2039
ASEAN	George Paine	3647	2032

Country	Desk Officer	Direct Dial Phone (202) 482-	Room
Asia (Central)	Pam Feodoroff	2042	3316
Australia	Gary Bouck/	3646	2036
	William Golike	3646	2036

B

Bahamas	Mark Siegelman	5680	2039
Bahrain	Christopher Cerone/	1860	2029B
	Claude Clement	5545	2033
Balkan States	Jeremy Keller	4915	4313
Bangladesh	John Simmons	2954	2308
Barbados	Michelle Brooks	2527	2039
Belgium	Simon Bensimon	5401	3039
Belize	Michelle Brooks	2527	2039
Benin	Debra Henke	5149	3321
Bermuda	Michelle Brooks	2527	2039
Bhutan	Timothy Gilman	2954	2308
Bolivia	Rebecca Hunt	2521	2037
Botswana	Finn Holm-Olsen	4228	3321
Brazil	Horace Jennings/	3872	3019
	Larry Farris	3871	3019
Brunei	Raphael Cung	3647	2032
Bulgaria	Jeremy Keller/	4915	3413
	Lynn Fabrizio		
Burkina Faso	Philip Michelini	4388	3323
Burma (Myanmar)	George Paine	3847	2032
Burundi	Philip Michelini	4388	3323

C

Cambodia	Hong-Phong Pho	3647	2308
Cameroon	Debra Henke	5149	3321
Canada	Jonathan Doh	3101	3033
Cape Verde	Philip Michelini	4388	3323
Cayman Islands	Michelle Brooks	2527	2039
Central Africa Republic	Debra Henke	5149	3317
Chad	Philip Michelini	4388	3323
Chile	Roger Turner	1495	3021
China (Southern)	Sheila Baker	3932	2317
Colombia	Paul Moore	1659	2037
Comoros	Chandra Watkins	4564	3323
Congo	Debra Henke	5149	3321
Costa Rica	Mark Siegelman	5680	2039
Côte d'Ivoire	Philip Michelini	4388	3323

Country	Desk Officer	Direct Dial Phone (202) 482-	Room
Cuba	Mark Siegelman	5680	2039
Cyprus	Ann Corro	3945	3042
Czechoslovakia	Mark Mowrey	4915	3413
D			
Denmark	Maryanne Kendall	3254	3037
Djibouti	Chandra Watkins	4564	3323
Dominica	Michelle Brooks	2527	2039
Dominican Republic	Mark Siegelman	5680	2039
E			
Ecuador	Paul Moore	1659	2037
Egypt	Thomas Sams/	1860	2029B
	Corey Wright	5506	2033
El Salvador	Helen Lee	2528	2039
Equatorial Guinea	Philip Michelini	4388	3323
Ethiopia	Chandra Watkins	4564	3323
European Community	Charles Ludolph	5276	3036
F			
Finland	Maryanne Kendall	3254	3037
France	Elena Mikalis	6008	3037
G			
Gabon	Debra Henke	5149	3321
Gambia	Philip Michelini	4388	3323
Germany	Brenda Fisher/	2435	3409
	John Larsen	2434	3409
Ghana	Debra Henke	5149	3321
Greece	Ann Corro	3945	3042
Grenada	Michelle Brooks	2527	2039
Guadeloupe	Michelle Brooks	2527	2039
Guatemala	Helen Lee	2528	2039
Guinea	Philip Michelini	4388	3323
Guinea-Bissau	Philip Michelini	4388	3323
Guyana	Michelle Brooks	2527	2039

Country	Desk Officer	Direct Dial Phone (202) 482-	Room
H			
Haiti	Mark Siegelman	5680	2039
Honduras	Helen Lee	2528	2039
Hong Kong	Sheila Baker	3932	2317
Hungary	Brian Toohey	4915	3413
I			
Iceland	Maryanne Kendall	3254	3037
India	John Crown/	2954	2308
	John Simmons/		
	Timothy Gilman		
Indonesia	Karen Goddin	3647	2032
Iran	Paul Thanos/	1860	2029B
	Kate FitzGerald-Wilks	4652	2033
Iraq	Thomas Sams/	1860	2029B
	Corey Wright	5506	2033
Ireland	Boyce Fitzpatrick	2177	3045
Israel	Paul Thanos/	1860	2029B
	Kate FitzGerald-Wilks	4652	2033
Italy	Boyce Fitzpatrick	2177	3045
J			
Jamaica	Mark Siegelman	5680	2039
Japan	Ed Leslie/	2425	2318
	Cantwell Walsh/		
	Eric Kennedy/		
	Cynthia Campbell/		
	Allan Christan		
Jordan	Corey Wright/	5506	2033
	Thomas Sams	1860	2029B
K			
Kenya	Chandra Watkins	4564	3323
Korea	Dan Duvall/	4957	2327
	Jeffrey Donius		
Kuwait	Corey Wright/	5506	2033
	Thomas Sams	1860	2029B

Country	Desk Officer	Direct Dial Phone (202) 482-	Room
L			
Laos	Hon-Phong Pho	3647	2308
Lebanon	Corey Wright/	5506	2033
	Thomas Sams	1860	2029B
Lesotho	Finn Holm-Olsen	4228	3321
Liberia	Philip Michelini	4388	3323
Libya	Claude Clement/	5545	2033
	Christopher Cerone	1860	2029B
Luxembourg	Simon Bensimon	5401	3039
M			
Macau	Sheila Baker	4681	2317
Madagascar	Chandra Watkins	4564	3323
Malawi	Finn Holm-Olsen	4228	3321
Malaysia	Raphael Cung	3647	2032
Maldives	John Simmons	2954	2308
Mali	Philip Michelini	4388	3323
Malta	Robert McLaughlin	3748	3049
Martinique	Michelle Brooks	4564	3323
Mauritania	Philip Michelini/	4388	3323
	Chandra Watkins	4564	3323
Mauritius	Chandra Watkins	4564	3323
Mexico	Rebecca Bannister	0300	3022
Mongolia	Sheila Baker	3932	2317
Montserrat	Michelle Brooks	2527	2039
Morocco	Claude Clement/	5545	2033
	Christopher Cerone	1860	2029B
Mozambique	Finn Holm-Olsen	4228	3321
N			
Namibia	Finn Holm-Olsen	4228	3321
Nepal	Timothy Gilman	2954	2308
Netherlands	Simon Bensimon	5401	3039
Netherlands Antilles	Michelle Brooks	2527	2039
New Zealand	William Golike/	3646	2032
	Gary Bouck	3646	2036
Nicaragua	Jay Dowling	1648	2039
Niger	Philip Michelini	4388	3323
Nigeria	Debra Henke	5149	3321
Norway	James Devlin	4414	3037

Country	Desk Officer	Direct Dial Phone (202) 482-	Room
O			
Oman	Paul Thanos/	1860	2029B
	Kate FitzGerald-Wilks	4652	2033
P			
Pacific Islands	William Golike/	3646	2036
	Gary Bouck	3647	
Pakistan	Timothy Gilman	2954	2308
Panama	Helen Lee	2528	3021
Paraguay	Randy Mye	1548	2039
People's Republic	Cheryl McQueen/	3932	2317
of China	Laura McCall	3583	2317
Peru	Rebecca Hunt	2521	2037
Philippines	George Paine	3647	2032
Poland	Audrey Zuck	4915	3413
Portugal	Ann Corro	3945	3042
Puerto Rico	Mark Siegelman	5680	2039
Q			
Qatar	Paul Thanos/	1850	2033
	Kate FitzGerald-Wilks	4652	
R			
Romania	Lynn Fabrizio	4915	3413
Russia	Tim Smith	0988	3316
Rwanda	Philip Michelini	4388	3323
S			
São Tomé and Principe	Philip Michelini	4388	3323
Saudi Arabia	Christopher Cerone/	1860	2029B
	Claude Clement	5545	2033
Senegal	Philip Michelini	4388	3323
Seychelles	Chandra Watkins	4564	3323
Sierra Leone	Philip Michelini	4388	3323
Singapore	Raphael Cung	3647	2032
Slovak Republics	Mark Mowrey	4915	3413
Somalia	Chandra Watkins	4564	3323
South Africa	Emily Solomon	5148	3321
Spain	Mary Beth Double	4508	3045

Country	Desk Officer	Direct Dial Phone (202) 482-	Room
Sri Lanka	John Simmons	2954	2308
St. Barthélemy	Michelle Brooks	2527	2039
St. Kitts–Nevis	Michelle Brooks	2527	2039
St. Lucia	Michelle Brooks	2527	2039
St. Martin	Michelle Brooks	2527	2039
St. Vincent/ Grenadines	Michelle Brooks	2527	2039
Sudan	Chandra Watkins	4564	3323
Suriname	Michelle Brooks	2527	2039
Swaziland	Finn Holm-Olsen	4228	3321
Sweden	James Devlin	4414	3037
Switzerland	Philip Combs	2920	3037
Syria	Corey Wright/	5506	2033
	Thomas Sams	1860	2029B

T

Taiwan	Ian Davis/	4957	2327
	Dan Duvall/	4957	2327
	Robert Chu	4957	2327
Tanzania	Finn Holm-Olsen	4228	3321
Thailand	Jean Kelly	3647	2032
Togo	Debra Henke	5149	3321
Trinidad and Tobago	Michelle Brooks	2527	2039
Tunisia	Corey Wright/	5506	2029B
	Thomas Sams	1860	2033
Turkey	Heidi Lamb	5373	3049
Turks and Caicos Islands	Mark Siegelman	5680	2039

U

Uganda	Chandra Watkins	4564	3323
Ukraine	Chris Lucyk	2018	2062
United Arab Emirates	Claude Clement/ Christopher Cerone	5545 1860	2033 2029B
United Kingdom	Robert McLaughlin	3748	3049
Uruguay	Roger Turner	1495	3021

Country	Desk Officer	Direct Dial Phone (202) 482-	Room
V			
Venezuela	Laura Zeiger-Hatfield	4303	2037
Vietnam	Hong-Phong Pho	3647	2032
Virgin Islands (British)	Michelle Brooks	2527	2039
Virgin Islands (U.S.)	Mark Siegelman	5680	2039
Y			
Yemen	Paul Thanos/	1860	2029B
	Kate FitzGerald-Wilks	4652	2033
Z			
Zaire	Philip Michelini	4388	3323
Zambia	Finn Holm-Olsen	4228	3321
Zimbabwe	Finn Holm-Olsen	4228	3321

APPENDIX C

International Organizations and Groups

This is a selected list of international organizations and groups that may provide assistance, create opportunities, or issue regulations that may affect your international business.

Andean Group (AG)

Established: 26 May 1969, effective 16 October 1969

Aim: To promote harmonious development through economic integration

Members (5): Bolivia, Colombia, Ecuador, Peru, Venezuela

Associate member (1): Panama

Observers (26): Argentina, Australia, Austria, Belgium, Brazil, Canada, Costa Rica, Denmark, Egypt, Finland, France, Germany, India, Israel, Italy, Japan, Mexico, Netherlands, Paraguay, Spain, Sweden, Switzerland, United Kingdom, United States, Uruguay, Yugoslavia

Arab League (AL), also known as League of Arab States (LAS)

Established: 22 March 1945

Aim: To promote economic, social, political, and military cooperation

Members (20): Algeria, Bahrain, Djibouti, Egypt, Iraq, Jordan, Kuwait, Lebanon, Libya, Mauritania, Morocco, Oman, Palestine Liberation Organization, Qatar, Saudi Arabia, Somalia, Sudan, Syria, Tunisia, United Arab Emirates, Yemen

Asian Development Bank (ADB)

Established: 19 December 1966

Aim: To promote regional economic cooperation

Regional members (35): Afghanistan, Australia, Bangladesh, Bhutan, Burma, Cambodia, China, Cook Islands, Fiji, Hong Kong, India,

Asian Development Bank (ADB) (cont.)

Indonesia, Japan, Kiribati, Korea (South), Laos, Malaysia, Maldives, Marshall Islands, Federated States of Micronesia, Mongolia, Nepal, New Zealand, Pakistan, Papua New Guinea, Philippines, Singapore, Solomon Islands, Sri Lanka, Taiwan, Thailand, Tonga, Vanuatu, Vietnam, Western Samoa

Nonregional members (15): Austria, Belgium, Canada, Denmark, Finland, France, Germany, Italy, Netherlands, Norway, Spain, Sweden, Switzerland, United Kingdom, United States

Association of Southeast Asian Nations (ASEAN)

Established: 9 August 1967

Aim: Regional economic, social, and cultural cooperation among the non-Communist countries of Southeast Asia

Members (6): Brunei, Indonesia, Malaysia, Philippines, Singapore, Thailand

Observer (1): Papua New Guinea

Bank for International Settlements (BIS)

Established: 20 January 1930, effective 17 March 1930

Aim: To promote cooperation among central banks in international financial settlements

Members (29): Australia, Austria, Belgium, Bulgaria, Canada, Czechoslovakia, Denmark, Finland, France, Germany, Greece, Hungary, Iceland, Ireland, Italy, Japan, Netherlands, Norway, Poland, Portugal, Romania, South Africa, Spain, Sweden, Switzerland, Turkey, United Kingdom, United States, Yugoslavia

Benelux Economic Union (Benelux)

Established: 3 February 1958, effective 1 November 1960

Aim: To develop closer economic cooperation and integration

Members (3): Belgium, Luxembourg, Netherlands

Caribbean Community and Common Market (CARICOM)

Established: 4 July 1973, effective 1 August 1973

Aim: To promote economic integration and development, especially among the less developed countries

Members (13): Antigua and Barbuda, Bahamas, Barbados, Belize, Dominica, Grenada, Guyana, Jamaica, Montserrat, Saint Kitts–Nevis, Saint Lucia, Saint Vincent and the Grenadines, Trinidad and Tobago

Associate members: (2): British Virgin Islands, Turks and Caicos Islands

Observers (10): Anguilla, Bermuda, Cayman Islands, Dominican Republic, Haiti, Mexico, Netherlands Antilles, Puerto Rico, Suriname, Venezuela

Caribbean Development Bank (CDB)

Established: 18 October 1969, effective 26 January 1970

Aim: To promote economic development and cooperation

Regional members (20): Anguilla, Antigua and Barbuda, Bahamas, Barbados, Belize, British Virgin Islands, Cayman Islands, Colombia, Dominica, Grenada, Guyana, Jamaica, Mexico, Montserrat, Saint Kitts–Nevis, Saint Lucia, Saint Vincent and the Grenadines, Trinidad and Tobago, Turks and Caicos Islands, Venezuela

Nonregional members (5): Canada, France, Germany, Italy, United Kingdom

Commonwealth (C)

Established: 31 December 1931

Aim: Voluntary association that evolved from the British Empire and that seeks to foster multinational cooperation and assistance

Members (48): Antigua and Barbuda, Australia, Bahamas, Bangladesh, Barbados, Belize, Botswana, Brunei, Canada, Cyprus, Dominica, The Gambia, Ghana, Grenada, Guyana, India, Jamaica, Kenya, Kiribati, Lesotho, Malawi, Malaysia, Maldives, Malta, Mauritius, Namibia, New Zealand, Nigeria, Pakistan, Papua New Guinea, Saint Kitts–Nevis, Saint Lucia, Saint Vincent and the Grenadines, Seychelles, Sierra Leone, Singapore, Solomon Islands, Sri Lanka, Swaziland, Tanzania, Tonga, Trinidad and Tobago, Uganda, United Kingdom, Vanuatu, Western Samoa, Zambia, Zimbabwe

Special members (2): Nauru, Tuvalu

Commonwealth of Independent States (CIS)

Established: 8 December 1991, effective 21 December 1991

Aim: To coordinate intercommonwealth relations and to provide a mechanism for the orderly dissolution of the USSR

Members (11): Armenia, Azerbaijan, Byelarus, Kazakhstan, Kyrgyzstan, Moldova, Russia, Tajikistan, Turkmenistan, Ukraine, Uzbekistan

Customs Cooperation Council (CCC)

Established: 15 December 1950

Aim: To promote international cooperation in customs matters

Members (108): Algeria, Angola, Argentina, Australia, Austria, Bahamas, Bangladesh, Belgium, Bermuda, Botswana, Brazil, Bulgaria, Burkina Faso, Burundi, Cameroon, Canada, Central African Republic, Chile, China, Congo, Cuba, Cyprus, Czechoslovakia, Denmark, Egypt, Ethiopia, Finland, France, Gabon, The Gambia, Germany, Ghana, Greece, Guatemala, Guyana, Haiti, Hong Kong, Hungary, Iceland, India, Indonesia, Iran, Iraq, Ireland, Israel, Italy, Ivory Coast, Jamaica, Japan, Jordan, Kenya, Korea (South), Lebanon, Lesotho, Liberia, Libya, Luxembourg, Madagascar, Malawi, Malaysia, Mali, Malta, Mauritania, Mauritius, Mexico, Morocco, Mozambique, Nepal, Netherlands, New Zealand, Niger, Nigeria, Norway, Pakistan, Paraguay, Peru, Philippines, Poland, Portugal, Romania, Rwanda, Saudi Arabia, Senegal, Sierra Leone, Singapore, South Africa, Spain, Sri Lanka, Sudan, Swaziland, Sweden, Switzerland, Syria, Tanzania, Thailand, Togo, Trinidad and Tobago, Tunisia, Turkey, Uganda, United Arab Emirates, United Kingdom, United States, Uruguay, Yugoslavia, Zaire, Zambia, Zimbabwe

European Community (EC)

Established: 8 April 1965, effective 1 July 1967

Aim: A fusing of the European Atomic Energy Community (Euratom), the European Coal and Steel Community (ESC), and the European Economic Community (EEC or Common Market); the EC plans to establish a completely integrated common market and an eventual federation of Europe

Members (12): Belgium, Denmark, France, Germany, Greece, Ireland, Italy, Luxembourg, Netherlands, Portugal, Spain, United Kingdom

Associate member (1): Czechoslovakia

European Free Trade Association (EFTA)

Established: 4 January 1960, effective 3 May 1960

Aim: To promote expansion of free trade

Members (7): Austria, Finland, Iceland, Liechtenstein, Norway, Sweden, Switzerland

General Agreement on Tariffs and Trade (GATT)

Established: 30 October 1947, effective 1 January 1948

Aim: To promote the expansion of international trade on a nondiscriminatory basis

Members (97): Antigua and Barbuda, Argentina, Australia, Austria, Bangladesh, Barbados, Belgium, Belize, Benin, Botswana, Brazil, Burkina Faso, Burma, Burundi, Cameroon, Canada, Central African Republic, Chad, Chile, Colombia, Congo, Cuba, Cyprus, Czechoslovakia, Denmark, Dominican Republic, Egypt, Finland, France, Gabon, The Gambia, Germany, Ghana, Greece, Guyana, Haiti, Hong Kong, Hungary, Iceland, India, Indonesia, Ireland, Israel, Italy, Ivory Coast, Jamaica, Japan, Kenya, Korea (South), Kuwait, Lesotho, Luxembourg, Madagascar, Malawi, Malaysia, Maldives, Malta, Mauritania, Mauritius, Mexico, Morocco, Netherlands, New Zealand, Nicaragua, Niger, Nigeria, Norway, Pakistan, Peru, Philippines, Poland, Portugal, Romania, Rwanda, Senegal, Sierra Leone, Singapore, South Africa, Spain, Sri Lanka, Suriname, Sweden, Switzerland, Tanzania, Thailand, Togo, Trinidad and Tobago, Tunisia, Turkey, Uganda, United Kingdom, United States, Uruguay, Yugoslavia, Zaire, Zambia, Zimbabwe

Group of 7 (G-7)

Established: 22 September 1985

Aim: The seven major non-Communist economic powers

Members (7): Canada, France, Germany, Italy, Japan, United Kingdon, United States

International Atomic Energy Agency (IAEA)

Established: 26 October 1956, effective 29 July 1957

Aim: To promote peaceful uses of atomic energy

Members (115): Afghanistan, Albania, Algeria, Argentina, Australia, Austria, Bangladesh, Belgium, Bolivia, Brazil, Bulgaria, Burma, Byelarus, Cambodia, Cameroon, Canada, Chile, China, Colombia, Costa Rica, Cuba, Cyprus, Czechoslovakia, Denmark, Dominican Republic, Ecuador, Egypt, El Salvador, Estonia, Ethiopia, Finland, France, Gabon, Germany, Ghana, Greece, Guatemala, Haiti, Hungary, Iceland, India, Indonesia, Iran, Iraq, Ireland, Israel, Italy, Ivory Coast, Jamaica, Japan, Jordan, Kenya, Korea (North), Korea (South), Kuwait, Latvia, Lebanon, Liberia, Libya, Liechtenstein, Lithuania, Luxembourg, Madagascar, Malaysia, Mali, Mauritius, Mexico, Monaco, Mongolia, Morocco, Namibia, Netherlands, New Zealand, Nicaragua, Niger, Nigeria, Norway, Pakistan, Panama, Paraguay, Peru, Philippines, Poland, Portugal, Qatar, Romania, Russia, Saudi Arabia, Senegal, Sierra Leone, Singapore, South Africa, Spain, Sri Lanka, Sudan, Sweden, Switzerland, Syria, Tanzania, Thailand, Tunisia, Turkey, Uganda, Ukraine, United Arab Emirates, United Kingdom, United States, Uruguay, Vatican City, Venezuela, Vietnam, Yugoslavia, Zaire, Zambia, Zimbabwe

International Chamber of Commerce (ICC)

Established: 1919

Aim: To promote free trade, private enterprise, and represent business interests at national and international levels

Members (58 national councils): Argentina, Australia, Austria, Belgium, Brazil, Burkina Faso, Cameroon, Canada, Colombia, Cyprus, Denmark, Ecuador, Egypt, Finland, France, Gabon, Germany, Greece, Iceland, India, Indonesia, Iran, Ireland, Israel, Italy, Ivory Coast, Japan, Jordan, Korea (South), Lebanon, Luxembourg, Madagascar, Mexico, Morocco, Netherlands, Nigeria, Norway, Pakistan, Portugal, Saudi Arabia, Senegal, Singapore, South Africa, Spain, Sri Lanka, Sweden, Switzerland, Syria, Taiwan, Togo, Tunisia, Turkey, United Kingdom, United States, Uruguay, Venezuela, Yugoslavia, Zaire

International Court of Justice (ICJ), also known as the World Court

Established: 26 June 1945, effective 24 October 1945

Aim: Primary judicial organ of the UN

Members: 15 judges elected by the General Assembly and Security Council to represent all principal legal systems

International Criminal Police Organization (INTERPOL)

Established: 13 June 1956

Aim: To promote international cooperation between criminal police authorities

Members (152): Albania, Algeria, Andorra, Angola, Antigua and Barbuda, Argentina, Aruba, Australia, Austria, Bahamas, Bahrain, Bangladesh, Barbados, Belgium, Belize, Benin, Bolivia, Botswana, Brazil, Brunei, Burkina Faso, Burma, Burundi, Cambodia, Cameroon, Canada, Cape Verde, Central African Republic, Chad, Chile, China, Colombia, Congo, Costa Rica, Cuba, Cyprus, Denmark, Djibouti, Dominica, Dominican Republic, Ecuador, Egypt, Equatorial Guinea, Ethiopia, Fiji, Finland, France, Gabon, The Gambia, Germany, Ghana, Greece, Grenada, Guatemala, Guinea, Guyana, Haiti, Honduras, Hungary, Iceland, India, Indonesia, Iran, Iraq, Ireland, Israel, Italy, Ivory Coast, Jamaica, Japan, Jordan, Kenya, Kiribati, Korea (South), Kuwait, Laos, Lebanon, Lesotho, Liberia, Libya, Liechtenstein, Luxembourg, Madagascar, Malawi, Malaysia, Maldives, Mali, Malta, Mauritania, Mauritius, Mexico, Monaco, Morocco, Mozambique, Nauru, Nepal, Netherlands, Netherlands Antilles, New Zealand, Nicaragua, Niger, Nigeria, Northern Ireland, Norway, Oman, Pakistan, Panama, Papua New Guinea, Paraguay, Peru, Philippines, Portugal, Qatar, Romania, Russia, Rwanda, Saint Kitts–Nevis, Saint Lucia, Saint Vincent and the Grenadines, São Tomé and Principe, Saudi Arabia, Senegal, Seychelles, Sierra Leone, Singapore, Somalia, Spain, Sri Lanka,

Sudan, Suriname, Swaziland, Sweden, Switzerland, Syria, Tanzania, Thailand, Togo, Tonga, Trinidad and Tobago, Tunisia, Turkey, Uganda, United Arab Emirates, United Kingdom, United States, Uruguay, Venezuela, Yemen, Yugoslavia, Zaire, Zambia, Zimbabwe

International Energy Agency (IEA)

Established: 15 November 1974

Aim: Established by the OECD to promote cooperation on energy matters, especially emergency oil sharing and relations between oil consumers and oil producers

Members (21): Australia, Austria, Belgium, Canada, Denmark, Germany, Greece, Ireland, Italy, Japan, Luxembourg, Netherlands, New Zealand, Norway, Portugal, Spain, Sweden, Switzerland, Turkey, United Kingdom, United States

International Monetary Fund (IMF)

Established: 22 July 1944, effective 27 December 1945

Aim: UN specialized agency concerned with world monetary stability and economic development

Members (156): All UN members except Armenia, Azerbaijan, Brunei, Byelarus, Cuba, Estonia, Kazakhstan, Korea (North), Kyrgyzstan, Latvia, Liechtenstein, Lithuania, Marshall Islands, Federation of Micronesia, Moldova, Russia, San Marino, Tajikistan, Turkmenistan, Ukraine, and Uzbekistan

International Organization for Standardization (ISO)

Established: February 1947

Aim: To promote the development of international standards

Members (72 national standards organizations): Albania, Algeria, Argentina, Australia, Austria, Bangladesh, Belgium, Brazil, Bulgaria, Canada, Chile, China, Colombia, Cuba, Cyprus, Czechoslovakia, Denmark, Egypt, Ethiopia, Finland, France, Germany, Ghana, Greece, Hungary, India, Indonesia, Iran, Iraq, Ireland, Israel, Italy, Ivory Coast, Jamaica, Japan, Kenya, Korea (North), Korea (South), Malaysia, Mexico, Mongolia, Morocco, Netherlands, New Zealand, Nigeria, Norway, Pakistan, Papua New Guinea, Peru, Philippines, Poland, Portugal, Russia, Saudi Arabia, Singapore, South Africa, Spain, Sri Lanka, Sudan, Sweden, Switzerland, Syria, Tanzania, Thailand, Trinidad and Tobago, Tunisia, Turkey, United Kingdom, United States, Venezuela, Vietnam, Yugoslavia

Correspondent members (14): Bahrain, Barbados, Brunei, Guinea, Hong Kong, Iceland, Jordan, Kuwait, Malawi, Mauritius, Oman, Senegal, United Arab Emirates, Uruguay

International Telecommunications Satellite Organization (INTELSAT)

Established: 20 August 1971, effective 12 February 1973

Aim: To develop and operate a global commercial telecommunications satellite system

Members (118): Afghanistan, Algeria, Angola, Argentina, Australia, Austria, Bahamas, Bangladesh, Barbados, Belgium, Benin, Bolivia, Brazil, Burkina Faso, Cameroon, Canada, Central African Republic, Chad, Chile, China, Colombia, Congo, Costa Rica, Cyprus, Denmark, Dominican Republic, Ecuador, Egypt, El Salvador, Ethiopia, Fiji, Finland, France, Gabon, Germany, Ghana, Greece, Guatemala, Guinea, Haiti, Honduras, Iceland, India, Indonesia, Iran, Iraq, Ireland, Israel, Italy, Ivory Coast, Jamaica, Japan, Jordan, Kenya, Korea (South), Kuwait, Lebanon, Libya, Liechtenstein, Luxembourg, Madagascar, Malawi, Malaysia, Mali, Mauritania, Mauritius, Mexico, Monaco, Morocco, Mozambique, Nepal, Netherlands, New Zealand, Nicaragua, Niger, Nigeria, Norway, Oman, Pakistan, Panama, Papua New Guinea, Paraguay, Peru, Philippines, Portugal, Qatar, Rwanda, Saudi Arabia, Senegal, Singapore, Somalia, South Africa, Spain, Sri Lanka, Sudan, Swaziland, Sweden, Switzerland, Syria, Tanzania, Thailand, Togo, Trinidad and Tobago, Tunisia, Turkey, Uganda, United Arab Emirates, United Kingdom, United States, Uruguay, Vatican City, Venezuela, Vietnam, Yemen, Yugoslavia, Zaire, Zambia, Zimbabwe

Latin American Integration Association (LAIA), also known as Asociación Latinoamericana de Integración (ALADI)

Established: 12 August 1980, effective 18 March 1981

Aim: To promote freer regional trade

Members (11): Argentina, Bolivia, Brazil, Chile, Colombia, Ecuador, Mexico, Paraguay, Peru, Uruguay, Venezuela

North Atlantic Treaty Organization (NATO)

Established: 17 September 1949

Aim: Mutual defense and cooperation in other areas

Members (16): Belgium, Canada, Denmark, France, Germany, Greece, Iceland, Italy, Luxembourg, Netherlands, Norway, Portugal, Spain, Turkey, United Kingdom, United States

Organization for Economic Cooperation and Development (OECD)

Established: 14 December 1960, effective 30 September 1961

Aim: To promote economic cooperation and development

Members (24): Australia, Austria, Belgium, Canada, Denmark, Finland, France, Germany, Greece, Iceland, Ireland, Italy, Japan, Luxembourg,

Netherlands, New Zealand, Norway, Portugal, Spain, Sweden, Switzerland, Turkey, United Kingdom, United States

Special member (1): Yugoslavia

Organization of American States (OAS)

Established: 30 April 1948, effective 13 December 1951

Aim: To promote peace and security as well as economic and social development

Members (35): Antigua and Barbuda, Argentina, Bahamas, Barbados, Belize, Bolivia, Brazil, Canada, Chile, Colombia, Costa Rica, Cuba (excluded from formal participation since 1962), Dominica, Dominican Republic, Ecuador, El Salvador, Grenada, Guatemala, Guyana, Haiti, Honduras, Jamaica, Mexico, Nicaragua, Panama, Paraguay, Peru, Saint Kitts–Nevis, Saint Lucia, Saint Vincent and the Grenadines, Suriname, Trinidad and Tobago, United States, Uruguay, Venezuela

Observers (25): Algeria, Austria, Belgium, Belize, Cyprus, Egypt, Equatorial Guinea, Finland, France, Germany, Greece, Guyana, Israel, Italy, Japan, Korea (South), Morocco, Netherlands, Pakistan, Portugal, Saudi Arabia, Spain, Switzerland, Vatican City

Organization of Petroleum Exporting Countries (OPEC)

Established: 14 September 1960

Aim: To coordinate petroleum policies

Members (13): Algeria, Ecuador, Gabon, Indonesia, Iran, Iraq, Kuwait, Libya, Nigeria, Qatar, Saudi Arabia, United Arab Emirates, Venezuela

United Nations (UN)

Established: 26 June 1945, effective 24 October 1945

Aim: A worldwide organization to maintain international peace and security, as well as to promote cooperation involving economic, social, cultural, and humanitarian problems

Members (175): Afghanistan, Albania, Algeria, Angola, Antigua and Barbuda, Argentina, Armenia, Australia, Austria, Azerbaijan, Bahamas, Bahrain, Bangladesh, Barbados, Belgium, Belize, Benin, Bhutan, Bolivia, Botswana, Brazil, Brunei, Bulgaria, Burkina Faso, Burma, Burundi, Byelarus, Cambodia, Cameroon, Canada, Cape Verde, Central African Republic, Chad, Chile, China, Colombia, Comoros, Congo, Costa Rica, Cuba, Cyprus, Czechoslovakia, Denmark, Djibouti, Dominica, Dominican Republic, Ecuador, Egypt, El Salvador, Equatorial Guinea, Estonia, Ethiopia, Fiji, Finland, France, Gabon, The Gambia, Germany, Ghana, Greece, Grenada, Guatemala, Guinea, Guinea-Bissau, Guyana, Haiti, Honduras, Hungary, Iceland, India, Indonesia, Iran, Iraq, Ireland,

United Nations (UN)   (cont.)
Israel, Italy, Ivory Coast, Jamaica, Japan, Jordan, Kazakhstan, Kenya,
Korea (North), Korea (South), Kuwait, Kyrgyzstan, Laos, Latvia,
Lebanon, Lesotho, Liberia, Libya, Liechtenstein, Lithuania,
Luxembourg, Madagascar, Malawi, Malaysia, Maldives, Mali, Malta,
Marshall Islands, Mauritania, Mauritius, Mexico, Federated States of
Micronesia, Moldova, Mongolia, Morocco, Mozambique, Namibia,
Nepal, Netherlands, New Zealand, Nicaragua, Niger, Nigeria, Norway,
Oman, Pakistan, Panama, Papua New Guinea, Paraguay, Peru,
Philippines, Poland, Portugal, Qatar, Romania, Russia, Rwanda, Saint
Kitts–Nevis, Saint Lucia, Saint Vincent and the Grenadines, San
Marino, São Tomé and Principe, Saudi Arabia, Senegal, Seychelles,
Sierra Leone, Singapore, Solomon Islands, Somalia, South Africa, Spain,
Sri Lanka, Sudan, Suriname, Swaziland, Sweden, Syria, Tajikistan,
Tanzania, Thailand, Togo, Trinidad and Tobago, Tunisia,
Turkmenistan, Turkey, Uganda, Ukraine, United Arab Emirates,
United Kingdom, United States, Uruguay, Uzbekistan, Vanuatu,
Venezuela, Vietnam, Western Samoa, Yemen, Yugoslavia, Zaire,
Zambia, Zimbabwe

Note: All UN members are represented in the General Assembly

Observers (4): Monaco, Palestine Liberation Organization, Switzerland,
Vatican City

World Intellectual Property Organization (WIPO)

Established: 14 July 1967, effective 26 April 1970

Aim: UN specialized agency concerned with the protection of literary,
artistic, and scientific works

Members (125): Algeria, Angola, Argentina, Australia, Austria,
Bahamas, Bangladesh, Barbados, Belgium, Benin, Brazil, Bulgaria,
Burkina Faso, Burundi, Byelarus, Cameroon, Canada, Central African
Republic, Chad, Chile, China, Colombia, Congo, Costa Rica, Cuba,
Cyprus, Czechoslovakia, Denmark, Ecuador, Egypt, El Salvador, Fiji,
Finland, France, Gabon, The Gambia, Germany, Ghana, Greece,
Guatemala, Guinea, Guinea-Bissau, Haiti, Honduras, Hungary, Iceland,
India, Indonesia, Iraq, Ireland, Israel, Italy, Ivory Coast, Jamaica, Japan,
Jordan, Kenya, Korea (North), Korea (South), Lebanon, Lesotho,
Liberia, Libya, Liechtenstein, Luxembourg, Madagascar, Malawi,
Malaysia, Mali, Malta, Mauritania, Mauritius, Mexico, Monaco,
Mongolia, Morocco, Netherlands, New Zealand, Nicaragua, Niger,
Norway, Pakistan, Panama, Paraguay, Peru, Philippines, Poland,
Portugal, Qatar, Romania, Russia, Rwanda, Saudi Arabia, Senegal,
Sierra Leone, Singapore, Somalia, South Africa, Spain, Sri Lanka,
Sudan, Suriname, Swaziland, Sweden, Switzerland, Tanzania, Thailand,
Togo, Trinidad and Tobago, Tunisia, Turkey, Uganda, Ukraine, United
Arab Emirates, United Kingdom, United States, Uruguay, Vatican City,
Venezuela, Vietnam, Yemen, Yugoslavia, Zaire, Zambia, Zimbabwe

APPENDIX D

Country Codes

This is a list of country codes for various countries around the world that support direct dialing from the United States. The difference between the local time and Eastern Standard Time is included. Remember to calculate the local time before you wake someone up in the middle of the night.

Country	Country Code	Principle City Codes	Time Zone (EST +/−)
Argentina	54	Buenos Aires, 1	+2
Australia	61	Sydney, 2; Melbourne, 3	+15
Austria	43	Vienna, 1	+6
Bahamas	809	Nassau, 32	0
Belgium	32	Brussels, 2	+6
Brazil	55	Rio de Janeiro, 21; São Paulo, 11	+2
Chile	56	Santiago, 2	+1
China (PRC)	86	Beijing, 1	+13
Colombia	57	Bogotá, 1	0
Costa Rica	506	San José, None	−1
Denmark	45	Copenhagen, 31, 32	+6
Ecuador	593	Quito, 2	0
Egypt	20	Cairo, 2	+7
Finland	358	Helsinki, 0	+7
France	33	Paris, 1; Marseilles, 91	+6
Germany	49	Berlin, 30; Munich, 89	+6
Great Britain	44	London, 71, 81; Glasgow, 41	+5
Greece	30	Athens, 1	+7
Hong Kong	852		+13
Hungary	36	Budapest, 1	+6
India	91	Delhi, 11; Bombay, 22	+10.5
Indonesia	62	Jakarta, 21	+12
Ireland	353	Dublin, 1	+5

Country	Country Code	Principle City Codes	Time Zone (EST +/−)
Israel	972	Tel Aviv, 3	+7
Italy	39	Milan, 2; Rome 6	+6
Japan	81	Tokyo, 3	+14
Korea, South	82	Seoul, 2	+14
Malaysia	60	Kuala Lumpur	+13
Mexico	52	Mexico City, 5	+1
Netherlands	31	Amsterdam, 20	+6
New Zealand	64	Aukland, 9	+17
Norway	47	Oslo, 22	+6
Panama	507		0
Philippines	63	Manila, 2	+13
Poland	48	Warsaw, 22	+6
Portugal	351	Lisbon, 1	+5
Romania	40		+7
Russia	7	Moscow, 95	+8
Saudi Arabia	966	Jiddah, 2	+8
Singapore	65		+13
Spain	34	Madrid, 1; Barcelona, 3	+6
Sweden	46	Stockholm, 8	+6
Switzerland	41	Geneva, 22; Zurich,	+6
Taiwan	886	Taipei, 2	+13
Thailand	66	Bangkok, 2	+12
Turkey	90	Ankara, 41; Istanbul, 1	+7
United Arab Emirates	971	Abu Dhabi, 2; Dubai, 4	+9
Venezuela	58	Caracas, 2	+1

APPENDIX E

Estimated Populations and Gross Domestic Products

The figures below represent the estimated population and Gross Domestic Product of each country as estimated by the Central Intelligence Agency as of February 1994. I have added the rank of each country relative to all other listed countries in each category (population, GDP, and GDP per capita).

Country	Population (Millions)	Rank	GDP $B	Rank	$ GDP per Capita	Rank
Afghanistan	16.1	51	3.00	91	186	96
Algeria	26.6	36	54.00	41	2,030	51
Argentina	32.9	31	101.20	29	3,076	42
Australia	17.5	48	280.00	14	16,000	17
Austria	7.9	73	164.10	20	20,772	3
Bangladesh	119.4	10	23.10	60	193	93
Belgium	10.0	67	171.80	19	17,180	9
Bolivia	7.3	75	4.60	85	630	73
Botswana	1.3	99	3.60	86	2,769	44
Brazil	158.2	5	358.00	11	2,263	48
Brunei	0.3	101	3.50	88	13,462	23
Bulgaria	8.9	69	36.40	51	4,090	37
Burma (Myanmar)	42.6	25	22.20	61	521	75
Cambodia	7.3	76	0.93	100	127	98
Cameroon	12.7	58	11.50	67	906	67
Canada	27.4	34	521.50	8	19,033	5
Chile	13.5	56	30.50	54	2,259	49
Colombia	34.3	30	45.00	47	1,312	60
Cuba	10.8	62	17.00	63	1,574	55
Czechoslovakia	15.7	52	108.90	26	6,936	30
Denmark	5.2	80	91.10	31	17,519	8
Dominican Republic	7.5	74	7.00	77	933	65
Ecuador	10.9	61	11.50	68	1,055	62

Country	Population (Millions)	Rank	GDP $B	Rank	$ GDP per Capita	Rank
Egypt	56.4	21	39.20	48	695	71
Ethiopia	54.2	22	6.60	79	122	100
Finland	5.0	81	80.60	35	16,120	16
France	57.3	20	1,033.70	5	18,040	7
Germany	80.4	12	1,331.40	4	16,560	14
Ghana	16.2	50	6.20	80	383	82
Greece	10.1	66	77.60	36	7,683	28
Guatemala	9.7	68	11.70	66	1,206	61
Haiti	6.4	78	2.70	92	422	78
Hong Kong	5.9	79	80.90	34	13,712	20
Hungary	10.3	65	60.10	39	5,835	35
India	886.3	2	328.00	12	370	85
Indonesia	195.7	4	122.00	25	623	74
Iran	61.2	15	90.00	32	1,471	56
Iraq	18.4	45	35.00	52	1,902	53
Ireland	3.5	88	39.20	49	11,200	26
Israel	4.7	83	54.60	40	11,617	25
Italy	57.9	17	965.00	6	16,667	13
Ivory Coast	13.5	57	10.00	69	741	69
Jamaica	2.5	93	3.60	87	1,440	57
Japan	124.5	8	2,360.80	3	18,961	6
Kenya	26.1	37	9.70	71	372	84
Korea, North	22.2	40	23.30	59	1,050	63
Korea, South	44.1	24	273.00	15	6,190	33
Kuwait	1.4	98	8.75	73	6,250	32
Laos	4.4	85	0.80	101	182	96
Lebanon	3.4	89	4.80	84	1,412	59
Liberia	2.4	96	1.00	99	417	79
Libya	4.5	84	28.90	57	6,422	31
Luxembourg	0.4	100	7.80	74	19,898	4
Madagascar	12.6	59	2.40	93	190	94
Malaysia	18.4	46	48.00	43	2,609	45
Mexico	92.3	11	289.00	13	3,131	40
Mongolia	2.3	97	2.10	96	913	66
Morocco	26.7	35	27.30	58	1,022	64
Mozambique	15.5	53	1.70	97	110	101
Nepal	20.1	42	3.20	90	159	97
Netherlands	15.1	54	249.60	16	16,530	15
New Zealand	3.3	90	46.20	45	14,000	19
Nicaragua	3.9	87	1.60	98	410	80
Niger	8.1	71	2.40	94	296	87
Nigeria	126.3	7	30.00	55	238	91
Norway	4.3	86	72.90	37	16,953	11
Pakistan	121.7	9	45.40	46	373	83
Panama	2.5	94	5.00	83	2,000	52
Paraguay	4.9	82	7.00	78	1,429	58

Country	Population (Millions)	Rank	GDP $B	Rank	$ GDP per Capita	Rank
People's Republic of China	1,169.6	1	393.00	10	336	86
Peru	22.8	39	20.60	62	904	68
Philippines	67.1	14	47.00	44	700	70
Poland	38.4	29	162.70	21	4,237	36
Portugal	10.4	63	87.30	33	8,394	27
Romania	23.2	38	71.90	38	3,099	41
Russia	149.5	6	2,500.00	2	16,722	12
Rwanda	8.1	72	2.35	95	290	88
Saudi Arabia	17.1	49	104.00	27	6,082	34
Singapore	2.8	92	38.30	50	13,679	21
South Africa	41.7	26	104.00	28	2,494	47
Spain	39.2	27	487.50	9	12,436	24
Sri Lanka	17.6	47	7.20	75	409	81
Sudan	28.3	32	12.10	65	428	77
Sweden	8.6	70	147.60	23	17,163	10
Switzerland	6.8	77	147.40	24	21,676	2
Syria	13.7	55	30.00	56	2,190	50
Taiwan	20.1	43	150.80	22	7,502	29
Tanzania	27.8	33	3.40	89	122	99
Thailand	57.6	19	92.60	30	1,608	54
Turkey	59.6	16	198.00	17	3,322	39
Uganda	19.4	44	5.60	81	289	89
Ukraine	51.9	23	195.50	18	3,767	38
United Arab Emirates	2.5	95	33.70	53	13,480	22
United Kingdom	57.8	18	915.00	7	15,839	18
United States	254.5	3	5,673.00	1	22,291	1
Uruguay	3.1	91	9.10	72	2,935	43
Venezuela	20.7	41	52.30	42	2,527	46
Vietnam	68.9	13	15.00	64	218	92
Yemen	10.4	64	5.30	82	510	76
Zaire	39.1	28	9.80	70	251	90
Zimabawe	11.0	60	7.10	76	645	72
World	5,515.6		25,000.00		4,533	

APPENDIX F

Bibliography

Axtell, Roger. 1993. *Do's and Taboos Around the World*. New York: Wiley.

Axtell, Roger. 1993. *Do's and Taboos of Hosting International Visitors*. New York: Wiley.

Axtell, Roger. 1989. *The Do's and Taboos of International Trade*. New York: Wiley.

Ball, Donald. 1993. *International Business: Introduction and Essentials*, 5th Edition. Homewood, IL: Irwin.

Barry, Dave. 1992. *Dave Barry Does Japan*. New York: Random House.

Buckley, Peter. 1992. *International Business Studies: An Overview*. Cambridge, MA: Blackwell.

Central Intelligence Agency. 1994. *The World Factbook 1994*. Washington, DC: Central Intelligence Agency.

Copland, Lennie and Lewis Griggs. 1985. *Going International: How to Make Friends and Deal Effectively in the Global Marketplace*. New York: Random House.

Currid, Cheryl. 1993. *The Electronic Invasion: Survival Guide for the Brave New World of Business Communications*. New York: Brady.

Currid, Cheryl. 1993. *Computing Strategies for Reengineering Your Organization.* Rocklin, CA: Prima Publishing.

Currid, Cheryl & Company. 1994. *Reengineering ToolKit: 15 Tools and Technologies for Reengineering Your Organization.* Rocklin, CA: Prima Publishing.

Cundiff, Edward. 1988. *Marketing in the International Environment,* 2nd Edition. Englewood Cliffs, NJ: Prentice-Hall.

Kelly, John M. 1987. *How to Check Out Your Competition: A Complete Plan for Investigating Your Market.* New York: Wiley.

Kotler, Philip. 1986. *Principle of Marketing,* 3rd Edition. Englewood Cliffs, NJ: Prentice-Hall.

Lareau, William. 1991. *American Samurai: Warrior for the Coming Dark Ages of American Business.* Clinton, NJ: New Win Publishing.

Nelson, Carl A. 1990. *Global Success: International Business Tactics for the 1990s.* Blue Ridge Summit, PA: Liberty Hall Press.

Ohmae, Kenichi. 1982. *The Mind of the Strategist: The Art of Japanese Business.* New York: McGraw-Hill.

Ohmae, Kenichi. 1990. *The Borderless World: Power and Strategy in the Interlinked Economy.* New York: Harper Business.

Ohmae, Kenichi. 1985. *Triad Power: The Coming Shape of Global Competition.* New York: The Free Press.

Porter, Michael E. 1990. *The Competitive Advantage of Nations.* New York: The Free Press.

Rodkin, Henry H. 1990. *The Ultimate Overseas Business Guide for Growing Companies.* Homewood, IL: Dow Jones Irwin.

Schmidheiny, Stephan. 1992. *Changing Course: A Global Business Perspective on Development and the Environment.* Cambridge, MA: MIT Press.

Walmsley, John. 1898. *The Development of International Markets.* Boston: Graham & Trotman.

Yoshino, Michael Y. 1975. *Marketing in Japan: A Management Guide.* New York: Praeger.

Index

ABNT (Associacão Brasileira de
Normas Tecnicas), 187
absorbing new technology, 3
A.C. Nielson and Company, 57–58
acceleration, of technology, 2, 3
accountability tools, 9, 47
ADB (Asian Development Bank),
215
advertising
agencies, 103
budget, 104
centralized approach, 103–105
comparative, 102
control issues, 104
cost considerations, 106
creative process, 103
decentralized approach, 105–106
documentation, 109–111
flexibility, 105
guidelines, 103
legal considerations, 102
management and cost, 105
worldwide coverage, 103–104
AEE (Asociacion Electrotecnica y
Electronica Espanola), 201
Aetna, jobs eliminated, 18
ALADI (Asociacion
Latinoamericana de
Integracion), 222
alphabets, Japanese, 66
alternatives, presented by change,
19–20
America Online, 61
American automotive industry, 19
American National Standards
Institute (ANSI), 203
The American Way, 147–149
Andean Group (AG), 215
antiboycott regulations, 95
Apple Computer
Apple Personal Computer (Apple
I), 2
market share in Japan, 145, 146

applications for global business
See enabling technologies
Applied Research Labs of Florida
(ARL), 203
Arab League (AL), 215
Argentina
duties on products, 119–120
indexing prices against U.S.
dollars, 140
standards and testing agencies,
185
ARL (Applied Research Labs of
Florida), 203
Asian Development Bank (ADB),
215–216
Asociación Electrotécnica y
Electronica Española (AEE),
201
Asociacion Latinoamericana de
Integracion (ALADI), 222
Associacao Brasileira de Normas
Tecnicas (ABNT), 187
Association of Polish Electrical
Engineers, 199
Association of Short Circuit Testing
Authorities, Inc. (ASTA), 203
Association of Southeast Asian
Nations (ASEAN), 70, 96, 216
ASTA (Association of Short Circuit
Testing Authorities, Inc.), 203
AT&T, jobs eliminated, 18
Attila the Hun, xii
Australia, standards and testing
agencies, 185–187
Austria, standards agency, 187
Avis, communications strategy,
99
Axtell, Roger, 179–180

Babbage, Charles, 2
Badan Kerjasama Standardisasi
LIPI-YDNI, 194
Bank for International Settlements
(BIS), 216
Bank of America, jobs eliminated,
18
banking industry, 20
bartering, 135